Christ, the One Sent

John P. Brennan, S.M.A.

D1521386

A Liturgical Press Book

THE LITURGICAL PRESS
Collegeville, Minnesota

To all missionaries,
especially my confreres in the
Society of African Missions (S.M.A.).

Cover design by David Manahan, O.S.B. "Head of Christ," by Rembrandt van Rijn (1606–1669), State Museum, Berlin.

The Scripture quotations are from the New Revised Standard Version Bible, Catholic edition, © 1989 by the Division of Christian Education of the National Council of Churches of Christ in the USA. Used by permission.

1	2	3	4	5	6	7	8

Library of Congress Cataloging-in-Publication Data

Brennan, John P., 1944–
    Christ, the one sent / John P. Brennan.
        p.   cm.
    Includes bibliographical references.
    ISBN 0-8146-2445-6
    1. Jesus Christ—Person and offices. 2. Mission of the church.
3. Catholic Church—Doctrines.   4. Catholic Church—Clergy.
5. Catholic Church—Membership.   I. Title.
BT205.B76   1997
232—dc21
                                                96-40324
                                                 CIP

Contents

CHAPTER 1

Who Do You Say I Am?

Jesus Christ stands at the very heart of Christianity not only as its founder but also as its ever present center. Without Jesus Christ there simply is no Christianity. He is the very source, the inspiration and model of life for Christians. As David Tracy puts it: "On inner-Christian grounds there is one classic event and person which normatively judges and informs all other Christian classics, and which also serves as the classic Christian focus for understanding God, self, others, society, history, nature and the whole Christian story: the event and person of Jesus Christ."[1] The essence, therefore, of the Christian way of life is to know this same Jesus Christ, whom we *now* experience as the exalted One, the Risen one, the One who lives and who is present to us. And it is to know Jesus Christ, not in any mere notional or intellectual sense, but in the sense of entering into a deep, personal, loving relationship with him.

From the experience of the saints, mediated to us through their own writings, and through biographies, we learn that it is profoundly enriching to have a deeper under-standing of the person of Jesus Christ, to enter ever more completely into the mystery of his being. However, it is not

---

[1]David Tracy, *The Analogical Imagination* (New York: Crossroad, 1987) 233.

merely enriching, it is to find salvation itself, to find nothing less than "the way, the truth and the life." Jesus invited his followers to come to know him better, to "come and see," to "follow" him. To know Christ in this true and deep sense is more than mere intellectual knowledge: it is to recognize and respond to his invitation to total commitment; it is to believe. Faith in Jesus Christ means that we hold as true that in him is manifested God's very self, and that he has manifested the self of God as the One who wills and brings about our salvation and that of all human beings; that God is indeed totally committed to the well-being of all persons and peoples; that in this God we find the meaning of human existence, for God is the supreme Meaning-Giver for men and women, and this is so precisely because the essence of God is Love, is to be Life-Giver. Only in God can our yearning for wholeness, for peace, for happiness, in a word, for salvation, find a response; only in this Holy Mystery that is God can we discover the authentic way of living, the one true mode-of-being-in-the-world. In God we discover indeed how to live, how to love, how to relate to this Holy Mystery that is the Godself, how to relate to others, to our world, how to be truly human.

It is also to acknowledge and accept that only by following Christ and through the power of his Spirit poured out upon us can we proclaim the one true God to the world. Consequently faith is ultimately the entrusting of our whole being to the God revealed in Jesus Christ. It is not mere intellectual curiosity that urges us to answer, or at least strive to answer, the questions of who Jesus is? What did he teach? What did he accomplish here on earth? What is his significance for us and for all other human beings? It is because these questions have an absolutely essential, vital, and eternal significance for each one of us and for all humanity.

In the Gospel of Mark we read the questions which Jesus posed to his followers: "Who do people say that I am?" (8:27) and "Who do *you* say that I am?" Christians of all eras and from all cultures must strive to answer these questions—and to do so from within their own specific life context. Nobody else can really answer the questions for us, neither philosopher nor theologian, neither scientist nor indeed the Church herself. All can help us to understand the question, to become aware of its significance, but only the individual can really *respond,* has the ability to respond to the question. Jesus doesn't ask anything peripheral, such as "what do you think of my message?" or "what is your opinion regarding the principles I proclaim?" but rather his question goes to the very heart of our stance before him: who is Jesus for me as an individual? It is a person-to-person question, one that involves the deepest levels of the beings of both. And the answer we give to that question will not only proclaim our understanding of who Jesus is, but will also proclaim our understanding of who we ourselves are, for in the measure in which I know who Jesus is, in that measure I also know who I myself am. In the mystery of Jesus the human being discovers his or her own most profound mystery, for in the mystery of Jesus we discover the mystery of God, the One and only Absolute before which all else is relative. Jesus has come forth from the mystery of God, through him in the gift of his Spirit we are led into that same Mystery.

Moreover, it is one of the convictions of Christianity that all seeking for the ultimate truth of human existence is a seeking for a Christology, a "searching Christology,"[2] to use Rahner's phrase. Before a person accepts Jesus Christ as God's revelation, the revelation of his Father, God's self-communication, there is a search for meaning, and in Rahner's opinion human beings are sufficiently conscious of what they are looking for to be able to recognize it when they find it. He says that in our search for salvation we seek for someone who can justify our belief that absolute love is possible, that despite the seeming absurdity of death, life has a meaning, and that in the end all will be well. All of us seek for the

---

[2]In this connection see Karl Rahner, *Foundations of Christian Faith* (New York: Crossroad, 1978) 295–98; also his essay on "Christology Today" in Karl Rahner and Wilhelm Thuesing, *A New Christology* (New York: Seabury, 1980) 3–17.

supreme fulfillment of our being, both in its individual and communitarian dimensions, and it is our faith conviction that in Christ we have the "unique supreme case of the total actualization of human reality."[3] The same theologian had remarked earlier in the same essay: "What do we Christians mean when we profess our faith in the incarnation of the Word of God? That is what we must try to say in ever new ways. It is the whole task of Christology, which will never be completed."[4]

In the two millennia which have passed since Jesus walked this earth, countless men and women have given their lives to him and for him, have tried to understand him, to enter into his character. As men and women inserted into that living tradition, we, too, if we are to give an adequate answer to the questions, must steep ourselves in the revelation that has been handed down to us from the apostles, and at the same time take into account the answers and attempted answers that have been given by our Christian ancestors down through the centuries. Our past walks with us and we stand on the shoulders of the Christian women and men who preceded us. They answered the question in terms that were comprehensible to them in their specific cultures and in their specific times. We must do the same for our cultural milieu and for our times. For example, in a former era the urgent question was: was Jesus fully human? Today, what is questioned is perhaps his divinity: Was Jesus truly divine? Our ancestors' way of phrasing the answer to the question will not necessarily be our way, but nevertheless, the process by means of which they arrived at their answer will be a guideline for us, alerting us to difficulties, pointing out to us possibilities, protecting us from misinterpretations, and enabling us in our day and age to be faithful to the whole deposit of revelation. Our theology is dependent on the faith passed down through the centuries by

---

[3]Karl Rahner, "On the Theology of the Incarnation" in *Theological Investigations* IV (New York: Crossroad, 1983) 110.
[4]Ibid. 105.

the Church, the Body of Christ, the Temple of his Spirit. The Good News, if it is to be vital and dynamic and relevant, must actualize itself in each generation and inculturate itself in each society and people.

It is particularly important for those of us who are called upon to proclaim Christ to others by word and example to be as clear as possible as to what we are to proclaim, even if we realize that all our proclamation must remain only partial, for if everything that could be said were to be said and written down, then "I suppose that the world itself could not contain the books that would be written" (John 21:25). In order to protect our proclamation from being distorted by the cultural environment in which we live and move, we must constantly steep ourselves in the original message. It is from that message that we derive our faith, our ultimate criteria, and if our praxis is to be right, then it must be constantly renewed and purified.

Missionaries (in the traditional and narrow sense of the term) are in a particularly difficult situation, for they must proclaim Christ to a people not their own, in a culture that is foreign to them in great measure, and very often in a language that they know only very inadequately. In a way, they share in a very concrete way the same challenge as the early Church and the authors of the New Testament. It is sometimes forgotten that the New Testament arose from a profoundly missionary Church and in response to a missionary need—the fact that it is written in Greek is sufficient indication of that—and many of the concerns to which it responds were concerns stemming from a specifically missionary context. For that reason it is vital for us to discover the missionary background of the New Testament and the specific influence that had on the portraits of Christ which it contains.

Right from the very beginning of Christianity, we find different understandings and interpretations of who Christ is and of what he did. In the New Testament we find many different Christologies: in each of the Gospel traditions, in the writings of Paul, in the Letter to the Hebrews, etc. and, as the

Biblical Commission's statement *Scripture and Christology* pointed out some years ago:

> These Christologies do not vary among themselves only because of the differing light by which they illumine the person of Christ as he fulfills the Prior Testament. But one or other brings forth new elements, especially the "infancy narratives" of Matthew and Luke, which teach the virginal conception of Jesus, whereas the mystery of his pre-existence is brought out in the writings of Paul and John. Yet a complete treatise on "Christ the Lord, Mediator, and Redeemer" is nowhere to be found. The New Testament authors, precisely as pastors and teachers, bear witness indeed to the same Christ, but with voices that differ as in the harmony of one piece of music. But all these testimonies must be accepted in their totality in order that Christology, as a form of knowledge about Christ rooted and based in faith, may thrive as true and authentic among believing Christians.[5]

In the Scriptures the different images of Christ presented by the New Testament authors are never identical, but rather each author presents a slightly different portrait of who Christ is for them and what is the significance of his work. I chose the word "portrait" in contradistinction to the word "snapshot," for a portrait strives to capture the essence of the sitter, to portray what the person is in himself or herself, while the snapshot usually is content in portraying what the sitter looks like externally. In the Gospels what we have are, as it were, different portraits (for the most part, in black-and-white, and in some cases, mere pen drawings!) by different artists of the one Person (but all inspired by the one Spirit!); portraits drawn with the primary purpose of facilitating the proclamation of their authors' faith in him, portraits that would help in the work of evangelization.

A good portrait artist may place the sitter in backgrounds that were unknown to the subject, or were even merely imagi-

---

[5]Joseph A. Fitzmyer, *Scripture & Christology. A Statement of the Biblical Commission with a Commentary* (New York: Paulist, 1986) 48–9.

native. But in doing so the artist hopes that the finished work better captures thereby the essence of the sitter, and the significance of the sitter for the viewer. In a somewhat similar way what we have in the New Testament are various verbal portraits of Jesus of Nazareth, written to help us capture his significance for our lives.

No two portraits are identical, and likewise no two documents of the New Testament portray Christ in identical ways. Indeed, to expect them to do so would be wrong, for what we have in the New Testament are summaries of faith experiences of Christ by different individual Christians and Christian communities, people who were guided by the Holy Spirit to meditate and reflect on the words and deeds of Jesus, and to do so in an ever deeper, ever richer, ever more developed manner. These were people with different community experiences and backgrounds and consequently people who saw Christ from slightly different perspectives.

Furthermore, faith is primarily a personal encounter between an individual and Christ, and every personal encounter between two individuals is unique, so again no two Christians will have identical portraits of Jesus Christ, but rather each will bring to the portrait a specific coloring, specific nuances, given by his or her family, community, education, life experiences, etc. Likewise the people for whom the portrait is destined will have an influence on the understanding of the finished work. For example, if the portrait is destined for Palestinian Jews or for Gentile converts then it will be affected by this change.

The different portraits of Jesus found in the New Testament are also due in part to the different experiences of the communities from which the various New Testament documents emerged.[6] Nevertheless, all the portraits are of the one Person, Jesus of Nazareth.

---

[6]On this point, see, for example, Jerome H. Neyrey, *Christ Is Community. The Christologies of the New Testament* (Wilmington: Glazier, 1985).

Finally, all the portraits speak in a powerful way to the person of faith. They were written from the position of faith to be found within the first Christian communities and it is in the community of faith—wherever it be found—that they find their natural resting place. Both the gift of faith and the gift of Holy Scripture come from the one Spirit. For this reason, *Dei Verbum* reminds us that "Sacred Scripture must be read and interpreted in the light of the same Spirit by whom it was written" (#12). Indeed, outside the realm of faith—gift of the Spirit—it is impossible to capture the essence of the person and work of Jesus Christ.

The faith of the first disciples is normative for all others, for these were the people who knew the Lord here on earth, who lived with him, heard his preaching, observed his miracles, shared food at the same table, and were witnesses to his death and resurrection. Our faith now in the twentieth century rests precisely on this witness of theirs. For that reason we say that our faith must be *apostolic*. The New Testament is first and foremost a record of the faith of the first apostolic community. It is customary to say that revelation closed with the death of the last apostle. This is true provided we remember that we are talking about revelation in the sense of what has been called "foundational" revelation. On-going revelation of God (based on this "foundational revelation") is an ever present reality, for God does not cease to communicate himself to us.[7] The final act of the work of salvation was the pouring out of the Holy Spirit on the world, and it was in this same Spirit that the Scriptures were written; it was in this same Spirit that the writings were recognized to be a reliable record of saving faith, and it is this same Spirit at work in the Church and in the individual that connects us in the one same faith of the apostles. It must likewise be remembered that the witness of the apostles is grounded in the Cross/resurrection of Jesus

---

[7]For the distinction between "Foundational revelation" and "Dependent revelation", see Gerald O'Collins, *Fundamental Theology* (New York: Paulist, 1981) 83–102.

Christ, so that in a very true sense it can also be said that public foundational revelation ended on Calvary, for there God committed definitively and irrevocably to humanity and to history.

Thus, in this little book what I intend to try to do is to present an understanding of Christ, his person and his work—for the two cannot be separated—as seen from the specific context of the missionary. I present it in the hope that it will be helpful to my fellow missionaries in their work of proclaiming Christ. I will try to present it as simply as possible, without shirking the difficulties involved in such an undertaking, for it is my conviction that any understanding of Christ that cannot be preached to the ordinary people in a language they can understand is not of much use, and is unacceptably elitist, a luxury that the Church can ill afford.

One may object that there is no need for yet another book on Christ, considering the veritable deluge of books and articles on Christology that have appeared in the past thirty years or so. However, the very multiplicity of the works on Christology would seem to indicate that the understanding of the person and mission of Christ is going through a crisis, at least for certain people. Many of the terms in which it was formerly expressed no longer speak to the modern mind, or do so, but without the same clarity or power as before. This has its repercussions on the missionary work of the Church, both on her direct and immediate agents of mission, and on the people to whom she wishes to proclaim the mystery of Christ. If I can contribute in some small way to facilitating the proclamation of Christ to others, to deepen, even if only minimally, the understanding of Christ's significance for each one of us, then I believe I will not have labored in vain.

Perhaps here at the beginning it might be helpful to state some of the presuppositions with which I work. No more can one just write of Jesus as we find him presented in the Gospels, as if each word and scene were derived from an audio-video recording of an actual event. The Gospels, as we know, are not biographies of Jesus in the modern sense of the term, even though it would appear that sometimes we have at the back of our minds the idea that in the Gospels what we have are indeed four different biographies of Christ. There are indeed biographical details in the Gospels, but they are not biographies! They are what they call themselves: Gospels! (from Middle English, *godspell*—good narrative, or good news). That is, they are proclamations of faith in Jesus Christ arising out of specific communities of faith, and aimed towards eliciting a response of faith in their hearers or readers. For that reason they do not give all the biographical details that we would perhaps like, but they strive to give what is essential to their purpose. This often leads them to select specific items, to condense others, so as to go to the heart of the matter in any particular event or in the overall event of Jesus Christ himself. When we read the Gospels as records of the Good News of salvation, and not as biographies or histories in the modern sense of the term, then we are protected against many misconceptions.

They are then, to repeat, first and foremost proclamations of the Good News of Jesus Christ written so that others may hear and respond to that Good News and in responding find salvation and become a sign and instrument of that salvation for others. They speak from a perspective of faith and are aimed at either eliciting faith or strengthening the faith of those who have already responded.

At the same time it must be stressed that it would be erroneous to imply that the Gospel portraits of Jesus are in any way false, a collection of fables, or that they are not entirely reliable. There are different levels of truth, and the Gospel portraits of Jesus are on a deeper level than that which can be recovered by mere historical research, (although that historical research is and will always be vitally important). As was pointed out above, the portraits are true and valid, but aimed at portraying the inner mind and spirit of Jesus rather than the more superficial, external details of his life—not that these are entirely lacking. Their aim is primarily rhetorical: to try and persuade men and women to enter into a *faith* relationship with this Jesus of Nazareth, and having entered into that relationship to continue to grow in it.

First, therefore, it is necessary to point out that while the New Testament is indeed a product of the faith of the early Church, this faith rests solidly on the historical experience of the earthly Jesus. Consequently, there is no separation, much less an opposition, between the Jesus of history and the Christ of faith.[8] Rather, the Jesus of history is discovered in and through the Christ of faith. One cannot talk about Christ at all without returning to the story of Jesus. The two—history and faith—are necessary. Faith is the necessary linking chain between us here and now and the Jesus who walked the streets of Jerusalem, making us part of that living tradition of the Church, binding us to the authors of the New Testament and through them to Jesus himself. Without faith there is no true, reliable access to the *Jesus* of history—but it is nevertheless a very true and real access to the Jesus of *history*. Faith is more than history and does not depend on history, but at the same time it cannot exist without some historical knowledge. "Faith is neither based simply on historical knowledge nor a mere prolongation of such knowledge, as though the critical investigation of history could by itself establish and maintain faith. Christian faith may not exist independently of historical knowledge, but it cannot be reduced to it."[9]

Here it may be helpful to recall the three stages which we find in the development of the Gospel narratives. First comes the stage of Jesus himself proclaiming the Good News by word and deed within his own specific Palestinian society. Secondly, comes the primitive Church recalling his

---

[8] It is not my intention here to enter into the theological mine-field that is the problem of the Jesus of History and the Christ of faith. For anyone interested I would recommend a careful reading of John P. Meier's *A Marginal Jew: Rethinking the Historical Jesus* (New York: Doubleday, 1991). See also, Edward Schillebeeckx, *Jesus. An Experiment in Christology* (New York: Seabury, 1979) 67–76; James M. Robinson's earlier work, *A New Quest of the Historical Jesus* (London: SCM, 1959) is still very valuable. James P. Mackey's *Jesus the Man and the Myth* (New York: Paulist, 1979) is also worthwhile, particularly pages 10–51.

[9] O'Collins, *Fundamental Theology,* 157.

words, remembering what he had done, and said, striving to understand and interpret all in the light of their experience of the resurrection. Finally come the evangelists who committed to writing aspects of this tradition for the sake of their contemporaries and future generations in the different Christian communities that were springing up throughout the Roman empire. Again, let us quote from *Scripture and Christology* of the Biblical Commission:

> But all these testimonies constitute for the faithful the unique gospel proclaimed by Christ and about him. No one of them can be rejected on the grounds that, being the product of a secondary development, it would not express the true image of Christ, or on the ground that, bearing the traces of a bygone cultural context, it would be of no importance today. The interpretation of the texts, which remains quite necessary, should by no means end up by throwing out any of their content.[10]

A faith that is not grounded in the historical person of Jesus of Nazareth runs the risk of becoming very quickly a mere ideology.[11] Likewise a Christology that is not based on the historical Jesus would be an insignificant mythological projection based on the subjectivity of its author. Take away either one of them—faith or history—and immediately you have a falsification of the reality. To maintain the dialectical tension between the two is essential if we are to acquire a true knowledge of Jesus Christ.

This is not to make undue claims for the historicity of each and every word or action of the Gospel portraits of Jesus, much less to claim that the New Testament gives us a literal account of all that Jesus said and did, but it is to claim that

[10]Fitzmyer, 49.

[11]Here I use the two terms "faith" and "ideology" in their traditional sense, although I agree with Juan Segundo that the two not only cannot be separated but are inextricably interconnected. See his *Faith and Ideologies,* vol. 1 of his *Jesus of Nazareth Yesterday and Today* (English trans., Maryknoll, N.Y.: Orbis, 1984).

the Gospels are reliable, trustworthy witnesses of the life of Christ, (even though at times we hear but a "whisper of his voice" and "trace in them but the outskirts of his ways"[12]) and that, therefore, the solid foundation of the Christ of faith as found in the New Testament is the historical Jesus. As Vatican II put it in its Dogmatic Constitution on Divine Revelation: "The Gospels . . . are our principal source for the life and teaching of the Incarnate Word, our Savior."[13]

Here we might recall the words of Jurgen Moltmann: "If we go back to the New Testament traditions we find that the history of Jesus Christ is always illuminated from two sides: it is narrated in the light of his historical mission, and it is recalled in the light of his eschatological resurrection."[14]

The quest for the historical Jesus was and continues to be important, but at the same time it must not be allowed to undermine in any way our appreciation of the whole New Testament canon nor the fact that *all* of this canon is inspired by God's Spirit. It is indeed important and helpful to know what came first and what last, what can be traced back to Jesus himself and what to the ecclesial community, but this does not imply that only the first set are inspired and the second set are not. The historical-critical method of interpretation has at times tended to emphasize the first aspect and neglect— or at least give the impression of neglecting—the second aspect.[15] The Bible, while being the work of human authors, is also the work of God. God is the "originator" *(auctor)* of all Scripture.

[12]R. H. Lightfoot, *History and Interpretation in the Gospels* (London and New York, 1935) 225.

[13]*Dei Verbum* 18.

[14]*Theology Today* (London and Philadelphia: SCM and Trinity Press International, 1988) 37.

[15]The benefits and dangers of the historical-critical method have been pointed out in the recent document (December 1993) of the Pontifical Biblical Commission, *The Interpretation of the Bible in the Church*. After recognizing that "the historical-critical method is an indispensable method for the scientific study of the meaning of ancient texts," it goes on to say that "no scientific method for the study of the

In this connection, we might also mention a related and obvious bias which developed with the use of the historical-critical method, namely the bias in favor of the earliest expressions of the tradition as being in some way purer and more authentic than the later expressions of the same tradition. But surely the later expressions, being the fruit of more mature, deeper reflection on the Christ event and the sending of his Spirit, and coming after a longer experience of the work of that same Spirit within individuals and within the community, are at the very least, as important, if not more so, than the early forms! The early Church had to struggle to find the language and concepts best suited for expressing the entirely new experience of God as mediated by Christ and the Spirit. The later and normally more developed stages of that struggle are to be found in the last documents to be included in the New Testament Canon. The earlier documents are necessary for the true understanding of the later one, and the later ones are necessary for a deeper understanding of the earlier ones. All are inspired by the one Spirit and together they form the witness of the apostolic faith upon which our own rests.

Also in connection with the 'quest for the historical Jesus' it might be helpful to point out that all historical writing involves interpretation, even the historical writing of the twentieth century! Each author of history has to impose some sort of narrative structure on the events to be related and this demands that the facts, the events, be interpreted in some way. Even to "video" an event implies the position of the camera, a point of view, the choice of images to be projected. If this is so for us in the modern era, how much more so for the writers of two thousand years ago! We must constantly strive to

---

Bible is fully adequate to comprehend the biblical texts in all their richness" and acknowledges that the "diachronic" approach of the historical-critical method needs the balancing of "synchronic" approaches and methods. The different methods and approaches do not exclude one another, but are complementary. The full text of the document can be found in *Origins,* CNS Documentary Service, vol. 23, #29 (Jan. 6, 1994).

bridge the distance between the world of the first recipients of the Scriptures and our contemporary world. This demands taking into account the "hermeneutical circle."[16]

Furthermore, as Franz Mussner pointed out many years ago, "A genuinely historical awareness cannot leave out of account its own present."[17] This is very relevant when one discusses the historicity of John's Gospel, for instance, but it is also important for understanding not only that Gospel but the whole New Testament, and for alerting us to the extent that our own interpretations of holy Scripture are conditioned. We too carry with us the unconsciously assumed presuppositions of our own age and culture. It is helpful, indeed essential for us, to examine both sets of presuppositions: those of the author we are discussing and our own.

While admitting that there are many portraits of Christ to be found in the New Testament, there is an underlying unity between them. They are all based on the one person of the Nazarene. This is not to deny that there are differences between the various portraits, but rather to proclaim their fundamental unity.

---

[16]Thanks to such thinkers as Hans Georg Gadamer and Paul Ricoeur we have become more aware of the mechanic of human understanding, especially when it is a question of understanding ancient texts. Here we might quote from the Pontifical Biblical Commission: "Gadamer . . . stresses the historical distance between the text and its interpreter. He takes up and develops the theory of the hermeneutical circle. Anticipations and preconceptions affecting our understanding stem from the tradition which carries us. This tradition consists in a mass of historical and cultural data which constitute our life context and our horizon of understanding. The interpreter is obliged to enter into dialogue with the reality at stake in the text. Understanding is reached in the fusion of the differing horizons of text and reader *(Horizonverschmelzung)*. This is possible only to the extent that there is a "belonging" *(Zugehoerigkeit)*, that is, a fundamental affinity between the interpreter and his or her object. Hermeneutics is a dialectical process: the understanding of a text always entails enhanced understanding of oneself." (PBC, *The Interpretation of the Bible in the Church II*, A.1).

[17]Franz Mussner, *The Historical Jesus in the Gospel of St. John* (London: Herder/Burns and Oates, 1967) 15.

Thirdly, to insist on a point mentioned earlier, it is of vital importance that we see the writings of the New Testament for what they are: the proclamation of the Good News of Jesus Christ. Faith in Christ is the heart and soul of these writings, faith confessed and professed. They witness to a faith lived, and at the same time constitute a vital proclamation of that faith to others.

This brings us to another point and one that is of equal importance, and that is that when speaking about God and the things of God we use language in a special way. We are using human language to express realities that infinitely surpass its capacity of expression. Thus our language is as it were metaphorical, or, as the theologians say, analogical. There is indeed an "analogy," a "relationship" between what we say and the reality signified, but there is never a one-to-one correlation. For example, when we talk about the resurrection, we are using a word to express a reality the full extent of which surpasses our ability to understand. Or when we talk about Jesus as the *Son* of God—with this term we struggle to express the reality that between Christ and the Father there is a profound relationship, a perfect and absolute love, a bond that is similar to the bond between a Father and Son—but at the same time infinitely surpasses that bond. Indeed, the dissimilarity is greater than the similarity! All theological language is basically analogical. This underlines the inadequacy of all attempts to describe the absolute mystery of God, because God surpasses in an infinite way our human categories. "God transcends all creatures. We must therefore continually purify our language of everything in it that is limited, image-bound or imperfect, if we are not to confuse our image of God—"the inexpressible, the incomprehensible, the invisible, the ungraspable"— with our human representations. Our human words always fall short of the mystery of God."[18]

In this context, it is helpful to point out that we must be careful not to make too sharp a separation between the work

[18] *Catechism of the Catholic Church*, #42.

of the exegete and the work of the systematic theologian.[19] Both are necessary, and both depend on faith. It is sometimes implied that the work of the exegete—particularly the practitioner of the historical-critical method—has little or nothing to do with faith, that it only has to do with the "scientific" investigation of the ancient texts. This is true, but only provided that the investigation takes place from the standpoint of faith. True Christian exegesis is as dependent on faith as is the work of systematic theology. For the exegete only fulfills the assigned task when Scripture is interpreted not only as the word of humans but primarily as the *word of God* and show how that word is vital and relevant for men and women of today. Exegesis is a *theological* discipline, for it too is *faith seeking understanding*.

Furthermore, it must be recalled that our faith does not depend on the work of biblical exegesis alone, but also rests on the personal experience of grace, on the lived tradition of faith down through the ages. The Spirit that inspired holy Scripture is the same Spirit that directed the Church in discerning the Canon of Scripture, and the same Spirit that is at work in the faithful in discerning therein the Word of God. This point too must be remembered not only by the systematic theologian but also by the biblical exegete.

This brings us to Christology strictly so called. Christology is the study of the person of Jesus Christ, and, since his person cannot be separated from his work, his activity, it also includes soteriology, or the teaching regarding the salvation which he brought about, and pneumatology, or the study of the Spirit, for the sending of the Spirit is the culmination of the work initiated in the sending of the Son in the incarnation. However, for study purposes we have to highlight particular areas (in our case, the person of Christ), but we should never forget the overall unity of the Father's plan of salvation.

[19]In this connection, see Karl Rahner, "The Position of Christology in the Church between Exegesis and Dogmatics" in *Theological Investigations* vol. IX (New York: Seabury, 1974) 185–214.

A high point in the theological understanding of Christ and his work—an understanding that sprung directly from faith as enshrined in Scripture and tradition—was achieved by the Church in the early councils, particularly those of Nicaea and Chalcedon. This is not to claim that the Chalcedonian "definition" is above criticism—and indeed there are certain aspects of it that no longer strike an immediate cord to our modern ears. For example, our modern world understands the term "substance" in a way that is almost exactly contrary to what the Fathers at Chalcedon wished to say, and even concepts like "human nature" are problematic, not to mention "divine nature" and how the two could possibly be united! Furthermore, its very abstraction seems to leave it wide open to manipulations of all sorts, and to a loss of contact with the historical Jesus.[20] Nevertheless, it does stand as a parameter within which we can continue our reflections on Christ with security. It has at least the virtue of clarifying what is to be rejected, even if what is positively stated about the incarnation remains obscure. Could it be otherwise? Chalcedon was both a point of arrival and a point of departure. It marks a certain stage in the understanding of the faith by the Church, but it also launches the Church into an ever deeper understanding of that same faith. It is a criterion by which we can judge if we are within the boundaries of faith, and a challenge to delve ever deeper in our efforts to understand and articulate it.

It is salutary to recall that the text of Chalcedon is written primarily in the *apophatic* or *negation* mode. In the Western tradition this is usually called the *via negativa*. This mode of doing theology emphasizes the fact that God is essentially unknowable, that all our words point to the absolute mystery that is God, that God can never be fully captured by any human word or human thought. Negative theology is not, however, a limitation on the mind. On the contrary, it is its liberation, constantly freeing human reason to continue search-

---

[20]Cf. John Sobrino, *Christology at the Crossroads* (Maryknoll, N.Y.: Orbis, 1978) especially, 4, 81, 330–2, 340–2, 386–8.

ing for an ever greater grasp of the truth, the truth that is none other than Jesus Christ: "the way, and the truth, and the life" (John 14:6). The *via positiva* or the *kataphatic* way of doing theology must always be immediately balanced by the *via negativa* or the *apophatic* way.[21]

It is important to remember that we stand within a *living* tradition, and as such the past must be inserted into the present in a true, vital way. We are not passing on a dead story of the past, but one that has to be retold anew in every age and place—for only thus does it maintain its vitality and relevance to the present, and only thus can it motivate us to seek and build a future that is coherent with this tradition. As Douglas S. Ottati has pointed out: "To stand in a living tradition . . . is to participate in a dynamic process of interpretation—one that moves between received heritage and the realities and challenges of the present world in order to express a continuing and vital orientation or identity."[22] And further on he writes: "(It) is to take the responsibility of shaping afresh the distinctive orientation of the Christian movement—of defining it anew for a given time and place."[23]

Finally, while taking the Chalcedonian "definition" (or better "description," as I do not see it, nor did it see itself, as putting any *finis*, any "end" to the mystery of Christ) into account, I do not intend to approach the subject starting "from above," from the trinitarian stance as it were, even though the Catholic tradition in theology has to a great extent used this approach; but rather "from below," from the figure of Jesus as he is portrayed for us in the Gospels and the New

---

[21]An interesting account of the importance of *apophasis* or *negation* in the theological enterprise among the theologians of the East in the early centuries, especially the Cappadocians, Basil the Great, Gregory of Nazianzus, and Gregory of Nyssa is found in Jaroslav Pelikan, *Christianity and Classical Culture* (New Haven, Conn.: Yale University Press, 1993).

[22]Douglas F. Ottati, *Jesus Christ and Christian Vision* (Minneapolis: Fortress, 1989) 5.

[23]Ibid. 5.

Testament generally, from the "historic" Jesus, to try and encounter Jesus as the first disciples did, taking his humanity seriously, his place in history, his cultural environment, and above all by a concentration on what he did, on what he saw as his mission. This approach is demanded by the anthropological shift in modern thought. However, it must be remembered that the two approaches—"from above" and "from below"—are ultimately interdependent: "Here are perspectives which mutually supplement each other. Both Christologies are to be related dialectically; otherwise we have a Christology without Jesus and a Jesuology without Christ."[24]

What we are underlining is our starting point, rather than any exclusion. We can only know Christ from what he did, from an examination of his mission. Strictly speaking, we cannot start from the being of Christ and then move on to examine his work for us. From our point of view, the movement is in the opposite direction: we start from what he did in order to discover who he was. Soteriology precedes Christology.

To know Christ is to come to know God the Father in the Spirit. Christology, pneumatology, soteriology, and trinitarian theology, and indeed all the other "tracts" in traditional Catholic theology, are all ways of relating to the one Mystery. However, more and more we are coming to realize that while it may be necessary, for pedagogical reasons, to study theology by dividing it into different "tracts," in doing so we run the risk of separating what should never be separated, and fail to see the vital interconnection and fundamental unity between them all. The Son of God and the Spirit of God are the two hands which invite and carry us into the one Holy Mystery that is God.

Furthermore, the deeper we enter into the mission of Christ—an entry made possible by the Gift of the Spirit—the deeper we discover his being, for his mission is the door into the mystery of his person, his relation to the Father, and so into the mystery of our own being as Christians. In reality, it

---

[24]Moltmann, *Theology Today*, 37.

is only by entering into and participating in the mission of Christ that we enter into and discover our own mission as Christians. Knowing Christ, discipleship of Christ, and Christian mission are to a certain extent synonymous terms. In other words, we become disciples of Christ only to the extent that we assume and make our own the mission of Christ, and we become missionaries of Jesus Christ only in the measure in which we become his disciples.

CHAPTER 2

Jesus, the One Sent

In the New Testament many techniques communicate the significance of Jesus Christ—who he is, what he does, and what he means for us. Usually the authors used images and symbols taken from their own religious past, but sometimes they adapted images and concepts taken from the Greek philosophical ambient of the time. The titles or names given to Jesus in the Gospels and by the Church down through the centuries are particularly significant in this regard. Thus we find titles such as Son of Man, Messiah, Mediator, Savior, Lord, the Word, Son of God, Good Shepherd, Living Bread, Vine, the Way, and others—each one trying to express something of the mystery of Jesus Christ.

Underlying all of this was the conviction that Jesus was *sent* by God for the salvation of humanity. The concept of "sending" is therefore an important concept for an understanding of Jesus, and one that is also of enormous importance for the understanding of our own vocation as Christians and especially our understanding of mission within Christianity. The idea of "sending" was not a new idea for the audience of Jesus, for it has its roots deep in the Old Testament.

The "Sent" of the Old Testament

Even a cursory browse through the Old Testament will bring out the fact that "sending" is central to God's way of relating to humanity as this is exemplified by his dealings with his chosen people. Right through the history of salvation God called individuals to be his envoys. At the very beginning of Israel's history stands Abraham, and he is presented as one sent by God:

> Now the LORD said to Abram: "Go from your country and your kindred and your father's house to the land that I will show you. I will make of you a great nation, and I will bless you and make your name great, so that you will be a blessing. I will bless those who bless you and the one who curses you I will curse; and in you all the families of the earth shall be blessed" (Gen 12:1-3).

Israel herself is chosen by God (a choice classically described in Deut 7:6-11) and sent by God into the world. Israel was to be the Servant of Yahweh, to stand before the nations as a light, pointing out the way to the true honor and worship of the one God. "You are my witnesses," says the Lord, "and my servant whom I have chosen" (Isa 43:10). This is repeated over and over again throughout the Old Testament, and especially in the so-called "Songs of the Suffering Servant" (Isa 42:1-7; 48:1-9a; 50:4-9; 52:13–53:12).

However, one of the perennial temptations of Israel was to be unfaithful to this aspect of their being sent to the nations. Repeatedly, God's chosen people was tempted to close in on itself, to constitute itself a closed club, a ghetto. In misguided attempts to protect itself from contamination, it very often ceased to be the light it was called to be. Israel sometimes understood its special call from God in terms of *privilege* rather than *mission*.

When we examine carefully the Scriptures, we find that the choice of God of any individual or nation is not to be understood in the first place as a privilege to be enjoyed, but as a task to be completed, a service to be rendered. The call is always for a particular purpose. Israel is sent to witness and to honor the name of the one, true God in the world. Through the celebration of her liturgy and the upholding of the law, Israel was meant to be a sign to the surrounding nations of the one, eternal, living God. Israel was to be a sign first and foremost by her way of life. As yet she does not see herself as sent positively out into the other nations, but rather to stand herself before them as a sign. Her testimony to Yahweh vis-a-vis the other nations is to be a testimony of life witness, rather than a testimony of word.

The role of the prophets likewise can best be understood in terms of their being sent by God to be God's special envoys, God's ambassadors before the people, to speak to them, instruct them, call them back to fidelity to the Covenant that they have entered into with Yahweh, that God has made with them. This idea is nicely summed up in the Book of Jeremiah: "From the day that your ancestors came out of the land of Egypt until this day, I have persistently sent all my servants the prophets to them, day after day" (7:25). Moses stands at the head of the prophets, an archetype of the prophetic vocation, called by name (Exod 3:4) and sent: "Come, I will send you to Pharaoh to bring my people, the Israelites, out of Egypt" (3:10).

He proclaims his unworthiness and begs the Lord: "Oh, my Lord, please send someone else" (Exod 4:13)—despite the fact that the Lord had assured him that he will be with him in the whole undertaking and therefore he should not be afraid: "I will be with you . . . ." (3:12). "I will be with your mouth and teach you what you are to speak" (4:12). However, God does not promise him any immunity from persecution, misunderstanding, pain or even, finally, death. Contradiction and suffering were to be part and parcel of his life thereafter. The call of Isaiah presents a similar pattern:

> Then I heard the voice of the Lord saying, "Whom shall I send, and who will go for us?" And I said, "Here am I; send me!" And He said, "Go, and say to this people . . . ." (Isa 6:8).

Again the call of Jeremiah:

> Now the word of the LORD came to me saying,
> "Before I formed you in the womb I knew you,
> and before you were born I consecrated you;
> I appointed you a prophet to the nations."

> Then I said, "Ah, LORD GOD! Truly I do not know how to
> speak, for I am only a boy." But the Lord said to me,
>> "Do not say, 'I am only a boy';
>> for you shall go to all to whom I send you,
>> and you shall speak whatever I command you.
>> Do not be afraid of them,
>> for I am with you to deliver you,
>>> says the LORD" (Jer 1:4-8).

The prophet Amos, who was clearly conscious that his role
did not come from birth: "I am no prophet, nor a prophet's
son" (Amos 7:14) was, however, at the same time very much
aware that he was sent by God: "The Lord said to me: 'Go,
prophesy to my people Israel'" (v. 14).

One of the distinguishing marks of the prophets is precisely
this awareness of having been sent by God, of speaking on
behalf of God, and an awareness that this commission to a
certain extent cut them off from the people, because it placed
them in a radically new relationship with God, a relationship
that they sometimes experienced as a heavy burden! As
Gerhard von Rad has remarked, "From the very beginning
not only the prophets' lips but also their whole lives were con-
scripted for special service."[1]

Furthermore, it may be noted here that another of the
characteristics of the prophets is that all of them had profound
personal experience of Yahweh in their lives. Sometimes this
is recorded as experiencing visions, or of Yahweh ordering
them to proclaim something.

The Wisdom Literature of the Old Testament is also instructive for the concept of sending. Wisdom "came forth
from the mouth of the Most High and covered the earth
like a mist" (Sir 24:3) and was sent by Yahweh to Israel:
"Then the Creator of all things gave me a command, and my
Creator chose the place for my tent" (24:8). The anthropo-
morphic expression of "sending" applied to God, underlined

[1]Gerhard von Rad, *The Message of the Prophets* (New York: Harper
and Row, 1962) 37.

that the task of the prophet did not arise in any way from the prophet's own initiative, or from his human ability. Whatever the true prophet said or did had to be understood as coming from God. Being "sent" was, as it were, the legitimation of the prophet's function, for who could dare speak on behalf of God, unless that person had indeed been commissioned to do so by God? This is further underlined by the prophet's speech beginning or ending with the phrase: "Thus says the Lord."

However, the "sending" is not associated only with the prophets, but right through the Old Testament we have numerous examples of God sending people for different purposes: Joseph, to prepare the ground for the entry of the Israelites into Egypt (Gen 45:5: "For God sent me before you to preserve life," and 45:7: "God sent me before you to preserve for you a remnant on earth. . . ."). We have the sending of Samuel to anoint Saul: "The LORD sent me to anoint you king over his people Israel" (1 Sam 15:1), and again he was sent to David: "I will send you to Jesse the Bethlehemite . . . ." (1 Sam 16:1). The same applies to the liberators of Israel, to Joshua: "Now proceed to cross this Jordan, you and all this people, into the land that I am giving them, to the Israelites" (Jos 1:2); Elijah (see 1 Kgs 19); Micai'ah (1 Kgs 22); the Judges, (see, for example, Ehud, Judg 3:15f.), Gideon, "Go in this might of yours and deliver Israel from the hand of Midian; I hereby commission you" (Judg 6:14). David likewise is sent forth by Yahweh on numerous occasions (2 Sam 5:19; 24:19; 1 Chr 14:10, etc.). In Israel, choice, election, always has to do with being sent by Yahweh for a purpose, a mission. The choice is not so much a privilege conferred upon a person or individual as a task confided to that individual or nation for the benefit of others.

Christ, the One Sent

In view of this Old Testament background, it is not surprising therefore that this notion of being sent should continue in the New Testament. It is a notion that the people would have no trouble understanding, and its implications would not have to be spelled out for them. The idea of Christ being *sent* comes through in varying degrees in all of the writings of the New Testament. In the Greek, there are two verbs used for "sending": *apostello* and *pempo*. *Apostello* is found some 135 times, while *pempo* occurs 80 times.[2] Let us look briefly at some of them. St. Paul, chronologically the first author in the New Testament, uses a variation of the verb *apostello* to help him explain his Gospel to the Galatians: "But when the fullness of time had come, God sent his Son, born of woman, born under the law, in order to redeem those who were under the law, so that we might receive adoption as children" (4:4).

We find the same idea in his Letter to the Romans:

> For God has done what the law, weakened by the flesh, could not do: by sending his own Son in the likeness of sinful flesh and to deal with sin, he condemned sin in the flesh, so that the just requirement of the law might be fulfilled in us, who walk not according to the flesh but according to the Spirit (8:3).

Notice how Paul here by using the phrase "his own Son" emphasizes the special bond of love and life that exists between the Father and the Son—a bond that is necessary for the fulfillment of the mission. Indeed, if the intimacy of the bond did not exist the goal of the "sending" could not be achieved. We will return to this point later.

In all four Gospels Jesus refers to his Father as "The One who sent me":

> Whoever welcomes you welcomes me, and whoever welcomes me welcomes the one who sent me (Matt 10:40; Luke 10:16).

> Whoever welcomes one such child in my name welcomes me; and whoever welcomes me, welcomes not me but the one who sent me (Mark 9:37; Luke 9:48).

---

[2]Gerhard Kittel, ed., *Theological Dictionary of the New Testament* (Grand Rapids: Eerdmans, 1968) 1:398f.

> Very truly, I tell you, whoever receives one whom I send re-
> ceives me; and whoever receives me receives him who sent me
> (John 13:20).

From an analysis of these texts exegetes have concluded
that the "sending" tradition of Jesus belongs to the very earliest tradition, and a tradition that deepened and developed
until it found its most perfect expression in the Gospel of
John. It can be seen as a key to the understanding of the
whole life of Jesus Christ. For example, Luke encapsulates the
entire ministry of Jesus in terms of his being sent by God to
proclaim good news, being anointed by the Spirit of God precisely for this purpose. For this reason Luke places the story
right at the beginning of the public ministry of Jesus.

> The Spirit of the Lord is upon me,
> because he has anointed me
> to bring good news to the poor,
> He has sent me to proclaim
> release to the captives,
> and recovery of sight to the blind,
> to let the oppressed go free,
> to proclaim the year of the Lord's favor (Luke 4:18-19).

One of the parables told by Jesus—and one that is found in
all three Synoptics—emphasizes the same point: the parable
of the Wicked Tenants: Mark 12:1-12, Matt 21:33-46; Luke
20:9-19. The parable tells of the "sending" of many servants
to the tenants of the vineyard, being rejected by the tenants,
and finally the owner sending his "beloved Son": "He had
still one other, a beloved son; finally he sent him to them, saying, 'They will respect my son'" (Mark 12:6).

There is obviously a parallel between the prophets sent by
Yahweh, and finally the sending of the Son, the last to be sent,
one that is essentially different from the servants by virtue of
the special relationship he has with Yahweh. It is of interest to
note that this parable in the Gospel according to Mark follows
immediately on the question, posed by "the chief priests, the
scribes and the elders": "By what authority are you doing these

things?" (11:28). In other words, the parable gives the foundation for the authority claimed by Jesus for his preaching and activity. He does what he does, says what he says, precisely because he is "the one sent." For that reason we can see the point of his remark quoted above from Matthew's Gospel: "He who welcomes me welcomes the one who sent me" (10:40).

To receive Jesus is to receive his Father. But likewise rejection of Jesus is rejection of the Father, rejection of God: "and whoever rejects me rejects the one who sent me" (Luke 10:16).

Matthew emphasizes the fact that Jesus saw himself as sent in the first place to the people of Israel: "I was sent only to the lost sheep of the house of Israel" (15:24).

Luke writes:

> I must proclaim the good news of the kingdom of God to the other cities also; for I was sent for this purpose (4:43).

However, it is in the Gospel according to John that we find the idea of Christ as the one sent most clearly enunciated. In John it is one of the key ideas in the elaboration of his whole theology.[3] It is, as one exegete puts it, the Gospel's "fundamental hermeneutic or leitmotif."[4] Indeed, in John's Gospel the expression "He who sent me" is so common that it constitutes a veritable substitute for the word "Father." It is also noteworthy that this affirmation of "being sent" is always found on the lips of Jesus. Some of the more important texts are:

> Indeed, God did not send the Son into the world to condemn the world, but in order that the world might be saved through him (3:17).

> Anyone who does not honor the Son does not honor the Father who sent Him (5:23).

---

[3]An important study on this theme is that of Josef Kuhl, *Die Sendung Jesu und der Kirche nach dem Johannes-Evangelium* (Sanct Augustin: Steyler Verlag, 1967).

[4]Teresa Okure, *The Johannine Approach to Mission: A Contextual Study of John 4:1-42* (WUNT 2,31; Tübingen: Mohr-Siebeck, 1988) 285.

Very truly, I tell you, anyone who hears my words, and believes him who sent me, has eternal life (5:24).

I seek to do not my own will, but the will of him who sent me (5:30).

The works that my Father has given me to complete, the very works that I am doing, testify on my behalf that the Father has sent me (5:36).

And the Father who sent me has himself testified on my behalf. You have never heard his voice, or seen his form, and you do not have his word abiding in you because you do not believe in him whom he has sent (5:37-8).

Then they said to him, "What must we do to perform the works of God?" Jesus answered them: "This is the work of God, that you believe in him whom he has sent" (6:29).

Everything that the Father gives me will come to me, and anyone who comes to me I will never drive away; for I have come down from heaven, not to do my own will, but the will of him who sent me. And this is the will of him who sent me that I should lose nothing of all that he has given me, but raise it up on the last day (6:37-39).

No one can come to me unless drawn by the Father who sent me (6:44).

Just as the living Father sent me, and I live because of the Father, so whoever eats me will live because of me (6:57).

My teaching is not mine but his who sent me (7:16).

You know me, and you know where I am from. I have not come on my own. But the one who sent me is true, and you do not know him. I know him, because I am from him, and he sent me (7:28-29).

Jesus said to them, "If God were your father, you would love me, for I came from God and now I am here. I did not come on my own, but he sent me" (8:42).

Can you say that the one whom the Father has sanctified and sent into the world is blaspheming because I said, "I am God's Son"? (10:36)

> I knew that you always hear me, but I have said this for the sake of the crowd standing here, so that they may believe that you sent me (11:42).

As we have seen earlier this use of the language of "sending" by Jesus was inherited from the Old Testament. However there is an important and vital difference between the "sending" of all others and the "sending" of Jesus. In all the others we have a determined moment when they are commissioned by Yahweh for the task that he wishes them to perform. We have already seen that in many cases they did not want the task, that they felt themselves totally unworthy of it, or incapable of fulfilling it. In the case of Jesus, however, there is no such moment of commissioning, no moment in which his mission is entrusted to him. On the contrary, his mission and his very being coincide. It is not so much a case of Jesus becoming aware of his mission, of his being sent by the Father, but rather the people becoming aware of it when he manifested himself to them. It was for this that John was sent to baptize: "I myself did not know him; but I came baptizing with water for this reason, that he might be revealed to Israel" (John 1:31).

Nor do we find any limitation in Jesus for the fulfillment of his mission. Jesus is not simply communicating a message; the very fact of his "sentness" has to be transmitted and believed:

> This is the work of God that you believe in him whom he has sent (John 6:29).

> . . . for the words that you gave to me I have given to them and they have received them and know in truth that I came from you; and they have believed that you sent me (John 17:8).

> Righteous Father, the world does not know you, but I know you; and these know that you have sent me (John 17:25).

It is presented as the aim of all his activity: "I knew that you always hear me, but I have said this for the sake of the crowd standing here, so that they may believe that you sent me" (11:42).

This is his prayer:

> I ask not only on behalf of these, but also on behalf of those who will believe in me through their word, that they may all be one. As you, Father, are in me and I am in you, may they also be in us, so that the world may believe that you have sent me (John 17:20-21).

John underlines the fact that the whole goal of the mission of Church is to know Jesus Christ, the One sent by the only true God: "And this is eternal life, that they may know you the only true God, and Jesus Christ whom you have sent" (17:3).

The number of these quotations could be further amplified by other verses from the rest of the Johannine corpus but I think these are sufficient to underline the point.

We now ask ourselves what significance for us has this insistence on the understanding of Christ as the one sent? Obviously, for the early Church, and especially for the Johannine community, it was extraordinarily significant, enabling them to interpret Christ for their own lives. For them Christ was first and foremost *the one sent by the Father for the salvation of the world.* In him, God and God's salvific will receive their supreme and ultimate expression. The Fourth Gospel brings out above all that Jesus is the *REVEALER* of the Father,[5] the *revealer of God,* the source and origin of all, of God who is Love, and the revealer of how humanity is to return to this same Father, this same God.

Jesus is in very truth the *Word* of God. In the fourth Gospel the theme of revelation is central. In this Gospel the Christology that we find in the rest of the New Testament comes to its completion, and it can indeed be presented as "the climax to the evolving thought of first-century Christian understanding of Christ."[6] Here the pre-existent, eternal Son

---

[5]See R. Bultmann, *The Gospel of John* (Philadelphia, 1971); also J.D.G. Dunn, *Christology in the Making* (Philadelphia: Westminster, 1980) 213–68.

[6]J.D.G. Dunn, *Christology in the Making,* 249.

of God, the Second Person of the Blessed Trinity, becomes incarnate, and in doing so manifests to the world the Father.[7]

The author of the Gospel had obviously spent many years reflecting on the words and actions of the historical Jesus, had experienced the presence of the Risen Lord in his life and in that of the ecclesial community, and was profoundly convinced of what we might call the vertical aspect of Christ's being and activity—he is the Word of God made flesh. But this awareness did not undermine his acceptance and conviction of the real-life historical Jesus from Nazareth who walked the dusty roads of Palestine proclaiming the Good News of liberation and salvation. When we read and study John's Gospel, we become aware that the portrait of Jesus that emerges is the portrait of him as he was experienced by the living, believing community. This does not mean that it is a purely arbitrary portrait, invented by the imagination of the author, but rather that it is a portrait painted by one who has experienced the Lord intimately, one who had entered deeply into the life of faith. For that reason the author feels free to present Jesus using the clearest expressions that will communicate what Jesus means for the believer.

Seeing Christ as the One sent by God helped to put the whole significance of Jesus into perspective for his community and for the communities who would follow. Let us look at some of the consequences of this description.

In the first place seeing Christ as the One sent by the Father underlines the fact that in the work of salvation all the initiative lies with the Father from first to last. Sometimes this can be forgotten, especially as we in the Western tradition have tended to place the whole emphasis in the plan of salvation on Jesus Christ. Indeed, the idea was somehow communicated that the whole economy of salvation was predicated of the Second Person of the Blessed Trinity alone! Yet Jesus

---

[7]He also reveals and manifests to the world the Holy Spirit. We will leave this point until chapter 8, but it is important that we try to keep in mind that Jesus is the revealer of *God* and that it is in Jesus that we discover the absolutely one God is a trinity of *hypostases,* of "persons."

himself constantly points the finger toward his heavenly Father, his "Abba." Jesus does not draw attention or indicate himself as the starting point or the endpoint of his mission, but rather points to the Father. Everything comes from the Father, *through* the Son, *in* the Holy Spirit and everything returns to the Father, through the Son in the Holy Spirit. For believers, Jesus becomes central precisely because of their awareness that in him we discover the Father:

> Jesus said to them, "Very truly, I tell you, the Son can do nothing on his own, but only what he sees the Father doing; for whatever the Father does the Son does likewise" (John 5:19).

And it is not only in his actions, in his miracles, but also in his preaching:

> For I have not spoken on my own; but the Father who sent me has himself given me a commandment about what to say and what to speak (John 12:49).

It must be remembered that for the early Church one of the first problems they had to confront was how to proclaim their full faith in Jesus Christ and at the same time not compromise their belief in one God. Absolute monotheism was an integral and unalienable part of their religious heritage and one that could not be compromised in any way, and this absolute monotheism was identified with the Father. The One God, *ho theos,* was understood first and foremost as being the Father. As Karl Rahner has pointed out, when the New Testament talks about God it is not referring to the three persons of the Blessed Trinity as one Divine Nature, but is referring directly to the Father, the First Person of the Blessed Trinity.[8] At the same time the first Christians experienced God in Jesus Christ, in his preaching and in his activity. The question was how to present this faith of theirs in a coherent and relevant

---

[8] See his "*Theos* in the New Testament" in *Theological Investigations* (London and Baltimore: Darton and Helicon, English trans., 1961) 79–149.

way without compromising either aspect. The concept of Jesus as the one sent by God—in the most profound sense possible—helped them to express their faith. Jesus is not a second God, but rather in and through him the one God and Father of all is present to the world and so belief in him is belief in God: "Whoever believes in me believes not in me but in him who sent me. And whoever sees me sees him who sent me" (John 12:44-45).

Here again notice the theme of Jesus as the revealer of the Father. This is so because the self-communication of God, the God who *is* love, the gift of God, is in Christ total and perfect. But the perfect and total self-communication of God in Jesus Christ did not destroy his humanity. The primitive Church had experienced Jesus as divine, and by the time of John's Gospel this was an established aspect of their faith. But they also knew him to be fully a man, one who shared their meals, wept over their sorrows, one subject to tiredness, frustration, suffering and death. He was really and truly a man, and Scripture proclaimed this from the beginning, but it also proclaimed that he was truly God. This was from the beginning, always has been and always must be the proclamation of the Church.

A powerful way of expressing this reality was underlining the special nature of his "sentness"—which brings out the distinction from the Father, and at the same time the identity of the Father with his mission: "Very truly, I tell you, whoever receives one whom I send receives me; and whoever receives me receives him who sent me" (John 13:20).

The special, intimate relationship of Jesus with the Father was no invention on the part of the author of the fourth Gospel. Almost all exegetes point out that all strands of the Gospel tradition testify to the fact that "Abba," was how Jesus usually addressed God.[9] Indeed, the word Father became the

---

[9]See Joachim Jeremias, *The Prayers of Jesus* (London: SCM, 1967) 54–57; also his *New Testament Theology I: The Proclamation of Jesus* (London: SCM, 1971) 62; James D.G. Dunn, *Jesus and the Spirit* (London: SCM, 1975) 21–40.

characteristic mode of address for the divinity in the New Testament and was not inherited from the Old Testament. It is calculated that in the Old Testament God is referred to as "Father" very rarely, not twenty times in all; but in John's Gospel alone God is referred to as "Father" some 115 times![10] The relationship between Jesus and his Father was profoundly dynamic and infinitely intimate. Later we will reflect on Jesus as the Son of the Father, but for the moment I want to emphasize the awareness of Jesus as the envoy of the Father.

The Envoy in the Israelite tradition

There is, in Hebrew, a special word for someone's personal envoy, or ambassador: the *shaliah*.[11] According to the Rabbinic school of thought, "The *shaliah* of a man is as the man himself."[12] While carrying out their mission, the *shaluhim* had all the authority of the person who sent them. The sender identified profoundly with his/her envoy, and the envoy's primary purpose was to "make present" the sender, to be absolutely faithful to the commission received. It is not recorded that Jesus ever called himself the *Shaliah* of the Father, (and indeed, the word *shaliah* is not found in written form until early in the second century[13]) even though he fulfills all the requirements for a *shaliah,* and obviously understood himself in this way. This was probably due to the fact that the concept is formally secular and legal, and also perhaps because the functions of the *shaliah* ceased when in the presence of his or her sender. Jesus was always aware of being in the presence

[10]See Gerhard Kittel and Gerhard Friedrich, eds. and Geoffrey W. Bromiley, trans., *Theological Dictionary of the New Testament* (Grand Rapids: Eerdmans, 1967) V:996.

[11]It is very close but not identical with the word "apostle."

[12]Thus the Rabbi Jonathan (ca. 140 B.C.).

[13]See Francis H. Agnew, "The Origin of the New Testament Apostle Concept: A Review of Research" in *Journal of Biblical Literature* 105:1 (March 1986) 75–96.

of his Father, and this is probably the principal obstacle to
his use of the word. However, this does not in any way pre-
clude the understanding of his mission as being that of envoyship, ambassadorial, and there is considerable evidence that
the *shaliah*-convention finds its origin in the Old Testament
period.[14] Some exegetes think that John 13:16 refers to this
shaliah-convention: "Very truly, I tell you, servants are not
greater than their master, nor are messengers greater than the
one who sent them."

When we look at Jesus as the envoy of the Father, the one
sent by the Father, as he proclaimed himself to be, we are reminded of the fact that Christ understood himself profoundly
as identified with the Father in all things and that likewise the
Father was identified with him in all things, in his very being
and in his activity. This is probably the first and most fundamental insight of the early Church into the mystery of Jesus:
his identity with the divine being and activity. From this insight
all the rest flows logically. It is the first step in Christology
properly so called. It is this awareness that makes him to proclaim—and the early Church to believe—that "The Father and
I are one." We have here that profound awareness of the relationship of Jesus to the Father as one that establishes distinction between the two, and one that paradoxically proclaims his
unity with the Father—an awareness that would take hundreds
of years to achieve full theological expression. To help us to
understand the "envoyship" of Christ we can reflect back on
the idea of being sent as it is found in the Old Testament.

Christ's self awareness was precisely his awareness of being
sent by the Father, and it was this awareness that molded his
response to each and every situation, this awareness that gave
him the courage and the strength to carry out his mission.
The Father is intimately within the work of salvation, not a
mere interested observer. Jesus comes to reveal to us the intimate being of the Father, a being that the inspired word of
Scripture would sum up with the word "love," and his will for

[14]Idem 85.

us. Moreover, he came not just to reveal it, to be a sign of it for us, but also to bring it about, to effect it. Sending forth is a reflection of the inner nature of God, of the inner dynamism, and as such it is the "natural" way of revealing the self of the divinity. For that reason Jesus precisely as the One Sent reveals the inner being of God.

In the life of Jesus the consciousness of being sent is what takes precedence over everything else: over his family, his comfort, his friends, his very life. From the moment that he assumed his mission on the banks of the river Jordan until his last cry on the lonely hillside of Calvary "It is concluded," his mission is uppermost. His whole life is total, complete dedication to the mission given to him by his Father. It is the guiding principle of all his words, all his actions, all his prayers. At times we can feel the powerful pull of this mission, this urge to move on, to bring the mission to its completion.

Taking cognizance of Jesus' awareness of being sent helps us to realize that the God revealed in Jesus Christ is Trinity. Rather than discovering Jesus in God, discovering Jesus present in the Trinity, we first of all discover God through Jesus. Jesus constantly refers everything to God, and this meant for him, the Father, including his own life and mission, and so while everything starts from the Trinity and finds fulfillment in the Trinity, it is the Jesus of Nazareth who enables us to see and appreciate this. In his relation to the Father he recognized the source of from which he himself flowed. This has important consequences for our Christology, for it is thereby placed within theology. Christ is understood most fully from within the Trinity, but the Trinity can only be known in and through Christ. For that reason, within Christianity there can be no rigid separation between theology and Christology.[15]

[15]Separating the two—as advocated by John Hick (in, for example, his *God Has Many Names,* London: Macmillan, 1980); Raimondo Panikkar (in *The Unknown Christ of Hinduism,* Maryknoll, N.Y.: Orbis, 1981); Stanley Samartha (in *Courage for Dialogue: Ecumenical Issues in Inter-Religious Relationships,* Maryknoll, N.Y.: Orbis, 1982); and Paul Knitter (in *No Other Name,* Maryknoll, N.Y.: Orbis, 1985) would seem

The Book of Genesis tells us that humanity is created in the image and likeness of God, and the God that is here referred to is the God of Jesus Christ, the God that is Trinity. However, it is sometimes forgotten that it is the same God that brings about humanity's redemption, and the image of that redemption is God as absolute, eternal love, the innermost nature of the divinity. Jesus came to bring us life in abundance precisely because he comes from life itself, the origin and source of all life. He came to bring us love—for he comes from the source of all love, and he revealed to us the nature of love in terms that we can understand, in terms of personal relationships, in terms of compassion, forgiveness, acceptance, peace, reconciliation. It is the being of the Sender that Christ reveals in his action, in his whole life, and that includes his death and resurrection. Indeed, it is precisely in his death and resurrection that he reveals most perfectly the Sender, Love itself, love that is prepared to give up the Only Begotten Son so that the adopted sons and daughters can have life.

The awareness of who we are, our self-identity, is one of the most effective forces in the carrying out of our mission in life. This applies to all human beings, and Jesus as a full human being is no exception (and let there be no doubt about the fullness of his humanity!). There has been a lot of discussion regarding the question of Jesus' self awareness, especially as regards the question of his knowledge of his sonship. How did he understand himself? Was he aware of his divinity? Sometimes such questions betray confusion in the mind of the questioner, who not rarely conceives of Christ's divinity and his humanity being somehow fused and expressed in one human understanding.

However, without going into the whole question of his consciousness, there is ample evidence in Scripture to suggest that he was profoundly aware of his envoyship, the fact that he was sent, and it was this awareness that gave him his sovereign liberty and his sense of authority vis-à-vis other people,

---

to be incompatible with Christianity. Yet all four work with an image of God that is derived almost exclusively from Christianity.

and even the law. Jesus must have had a true *human* self-awareness of who he was—and this human awareness of his divine origin finds expression precisely in his awareness of being sent, of coming from God, the God that he understood in the most profound way to be his *Father*. And paradoxically enough, this profound conviction of being sent by the Father, of coming from the Father, found its natural and perfect expression in his complete obedience to the Father, his total submission to the will of the Father. To be in any way disobedient to the Father would be a denial of who he was at the most profound level, a denial of his Sonship. God the Father is primordial Being, the source of all divinity and as total and complete outpouring of self, Jesus Christ is his Son, an outpouring that is effected in his Spirit. Apart from this pouring out of the self to the Son in the Spirit, God the Father would be totally inaccessible, it would be impossible to know anything of the inner nature of God.

It was this that gave Jesus Christ his profound freedom. Jesus knew that the institution of the law had indeed its origin in God, but at the same time he, as the "Son" of God in the most profound way, *homoousios* with him, felt qualified to bring the law to its fullness, to draw out its ultimate consequences even though this meant, in effect, abrogating some of its historical applications. As God's envoy, he knows that his authority is none other than the authority of God: "But I say to you . . . ." His relationship with God as revealed in his envoyship, his being sent, is primarily one of *communion*, sharing in life, rather than dependence.

The concept of "being sent by God"—as that is exemplified in the unique case of Jesus Christ—underlines therefore the aspect of relationship and as such helps us to understand what was the essential core of the later theological thinking on *person* as applied to Christ and to the Trinity.[16] In Trinitarian theology and in Christology person means fundamentally relation.

---

[16]See Joseph Ratzinger, "Concerning the Notion of Person in Theology," *Communio* 17 (Fall 1990) 439–54.

God the Father is *person* in the sense that God is always self-communicating. God is eternally giving Godself, eternally self-donation, eternally in a situation of relationship to others, a relationship that is one of total self-giving, total love. God is one on the level of substance, but on the level of dialogical relationship God is three. For that reason Jesus can stress that of himself he can do nothing (John 5:19), for the very reason that of himself *alone* as a relationship he has nothing, everything that he is and has is from the Father, but precisely within the relationship with the Father—because from him he has received all, he can say, "I and the Father are one" (John 10:30). The "sentness" of Jesus Christ underlines this aspect of *relationship*. What makes a person to be a person is precisely to be in relationship to others. In Scripture the complete revelation of what is meant by a person is total and perfect relationality—and this is found in God alone.

Let us return very briefly to the question of Christ's consciousness. To what extent was Jesus humanly aware of his divine nature? Or more simply, did Jesus know he was God? However, as Raymond Brown pointed out some years ago,[17] from a biblical point of view, the question cannot be answered. There is not sufficient historical evidence to ascertain to what extent Jesus was able to discern and express the mystery of his own being.[18] This is not to deny that he had it, but it is to say

---

[17]Raymond E. Brown, "Did Jesus Know He Was God?" *Biblical Theology Bulletin* XV, 74–9.

[18]Here we might recall the words of the Pontifical Biblical Commission in its *Statement on Scripture and Christology* (1984). Referring to the individual personality of Jesus it writes: "This individual personality was cultivated and formed by a Jewish education, the positive values of which Jesus took fully to himself. But it was also endowed with *a quite singular consciousness of himself*, as far as his relation to God was concerned as well as the mission he was to carry out for human beings. Some Gospel texts (e.g., Luke 2:40, 52) lead us to recognize a certain *growth* in this consciousness.

Nevertheless, (these) exegetes and theologians refuse to get involved in a "psychology" of Jesus, both because of critical problems in the texts and because of the danger of speculating (in some wrong way, either by

that we cannot assert to what extent he did have it, and in what terms he might articulate it. From the biblical evidence it can be seen that Jesus did have a profound awareness of his special and unique relationship with the Father, a relationship which he saw as justifying his authority, an authority which amazed his contemporaries (Mark 1:25). This relationship is evidenced in his words and deeds, even if it wasn't immediately perceived by all. And it was this that enabled the early Church to affirm their faith that in Jesus God was present. They had come to realize through their experience of Jesus that it was as correct to call him "God" as it was to call the Father in Heaven "God." Brown points out that "a teaching that Jesus knew his divine identity does not necessarily include a teaching that he would have been able to phrase this identity."[19] Divine knowledge in the strict sense could not be operative in a human mind.[20] Karl Rahner in his famous essay on "The Knowledge and Self-Consciousness of Christ"[21] talks about the "multi-layered structure" of knowledge and this means "that it is absolutely possible that in relation to these different dimensions of consciousness and knowledge something may be known and not known at the same time."

---

excess or by defect). They prefer a reverent circumspection before the mystery of his personality. Jesus took no pains to define it precisely, even though through his sayings or his deeds he did allow one to catch a mere glimpse of the secrets of his intimate life" (1.1.11.3). The text of the *Statement* with a commentary by Joseph A. Fitzmyer, S.J., was published by Paulist, 1986.

[19] Brown, "Did Jesus Know He Was God?" 75.

[20] See Thomas Aquinas, *Summa Theologiae* III, q. 1 ad 1, especially: "Christ knew everything by divine knowledge, through an uncreated operation which is the divine essence itself: for God's act of understanding is his very substance, as is proved in the *Metaphysics*. This act, then, could not be an act of the human soul of Christ, since it belongs to a different nature. If therefore there were no knowledge in the soul of Christ other than the divine, *it would have known nothing*. In that case it would be futile to have assumed it, since *a thing exists in order to operate*" (vol. 49, pp 84–7 of the English Dominicans edition, London, Blackfriars, 1974, Italics mine).

[21] *Theological Investigations* V, 199–211.

It is our firm faith that in Jesus Christ God manifests himself directly to us, and through him enters into a new and definitive relationship with us. However, it is likewise our firm faith that this same Jesus is not only the eternal Son of the Father, he is also a true human being, one in whom human nature is entirely restored, and transformed by the gracious presence of God. Jesus was present to himself, and that which is most peculiarly his as the Second Person of the Blessed Trinity, is precisely his "sentness," his relation to the Father and the Spirit. Within the heart of the Trinity the Father is as it were eternally "sending forth" the Son in an inexpressible movement of love.

It is this inner dynamism of God that is the cause and origin of all that exists, of creation in its entirety. Creation can be imaged as the external manifestation of the inner being of God, the external sign of the inward reality of God. Creation is therefore a sacrament (understood in the broad sense) of God, a sacrament that came to its absolute perfection in Christ. For that reason the act of creation is presented to us in Scripture as God breathing forth his word over the void, sending forth his word into the emptiness, the nothingness (and here we realize the inadequacy of language, and its analogical nature in theology) and thereby bringing the universe into existence. "Then God said, 'Let there be light'; and there was light" (Gen 1:3). "In the beginning was the Word, and the Word was with God, and the Word was God. He was in the beginning with God. All things came into being through him, and without him not one thing came into being" (John 1:1-3). This is not to say that the incarnation did not add anything radically new to the revelation initiated in creation. On the contrary. The revelation of God in creation—and indeed, the revelation of God in the Old Testament—without Christ would be radically incomprehensible. Christ opened the door to all previous aspects of God's self-revelation. The full significance of all previous revelation, its universal application and its transcendent reach, would be inaccessible without Christ. He is radically new, unimaginable and unthought of, and at the same time consonant with all that went before him.

It could not be otherwise, for all aspects of the Word have their origin in God.

Another aspect—and one that is important from a missionary point of view—is that Jesus constantly emphasizes that his being sent is for the whole world. Jesus, "the true light, which enlightens everyone was coming into the world" (John 1:9) and whatever he hears from the Father, he "declares to the world" (8:26). The message of Jesus is not for one small group, nor for one country or race but for all. He, as the Revealer of the mystery of the Father, is for all. He does not speak in secret: "I have spoken openly to the world; I have always taught in synagogues and in the temple, where all the Jews come together. I have said nothing in secret" (John 18:20).

The Good News of Jesus is not for some privileged group alone, not a secret to be shared only among a select band of initiates, but on the contrary is a message for the whole human race. The fact that not all will hear the message, that not all will respond to it positively, does not mean that it is not meant for them. Jesus himself constantly emphasizes that his message is to be proclaimed from the housetops that his followers are to be the light of the *world.*

The Lord Jesus, therefore, sums up in his own person all the "sendings" of God, the sending revealed in creation, the sending revealed in the call of Abraham and the call of Israel, the sending revealed in the prophets, the liberators, the kings of Israel—all find their maximum and most complete expression in him. Jesus, as it were, recapitulates in his own person all that preceded him and all that will follow. For that reason he is God's most perfect revelation, God's most perfect envoy, God's most perfect king, prophet, and liberator. And, as we shall see, as the Revealer of God, the One who sends, it is only fitting that he too becomes the perfect Sender of his Church.

Some may ask, if the concept of Christ as *the one sent* is so important how can we explain its relative neglect in the history of theology, at least in its Western expression. I feel that the reason is twofold. First, the first great faith struggle that the early Church had was with Arianism. Arianism denied the full divinity of Christ, subordinating him to the Father. One of the arguments they used was that the idea of "sending" implied an inferior relationship of the sent vis-à-vis the sender; therefore Christ must be inferior to the Father. It was shown by the great councils of the Church, especially Nicaea and Chalcedon that the sentness of the Second Person of the Blessed Trinity is from all eternity, is perfect.

When God communicates Godself, that means that the self of God is communicated perfectly, infinitely, otherwise it would not be *self*-communication. For that reason the Council of Nicaea declared that the nature of the Son was identical with the nature of the Father; the Son was *homoousios* with the Father. The difference lies not on the level of *ousios* /being /nature, but on the level of relationship/person/*hypostasis*. However, because of this abuse of the scriptural term "sent" the Church, and particularly the Western Church, which was always a little wary of anything that might compromise clear monotheism, tended to avoid the term for fear of misunderstanding. Thanks be to God that in recent years there has been a rediscovery of the vital importance of this term for an insight into God. The Christian understanding of God is Trinity, and this understanding must form the absolute foundation upon which everything else is built. Karl Rahner in his famous work on the Trinity pointed out that in actual fact "Christians are, in their practical life, almost mere 'monotheists.'"[22] One of the ways to rectify this is to rediscover the centrality of the "sentness" of Christ. It is noteworthy that the Second Vatican Council referred to Jesus Christ as the *One Sent* on numerous occasions.[23] Indeed it is the council's favorite title for Christ when referring to his saving mission.

Seeing Christ as the One Sent is of vital importance to us in the modern world. It is of supreme importance to rediscover

[22] *The Trinity* (London: Burns & Oates, 1970) 11.
[23] E.g., *Lumen gentium* 3, 13, 17, 18, 28; *Dei Verbum* 4; *Sacrosanctum concilium* 5, 6, 9, 24; *Presbyterorum ordinis* 2, 3, 8, 12; *Apostolicam actuositatem* 4; *Ad gentes* 3, 13.

God the Father as the absolute source of all that is and all that we are. Jesus reveals to us that this absolute source of our being is total, unconditional love; that God is not infinite egoism, infinite aloneness—but rather that God is infinite community, infinite relationship, infinite Love, Love that pours itself out, Love that is totally received, Love that binds the Lover infinitely and perfectly with the Beloved. This is the life of God and this is the Life into which we are invited, an invitation that Jesus Christ in his Spirit makes possible.

There is consequently a vital need for the Church to assume her full missionary role in the world, for all Christians to rediscover their *"sentness"* by God, and a first step in that direction is to rediscover Christ's "sentness." This "sentness" manifested itself in many ways and many terms were used to try and capture its significance for us and for our understanding of Christ. In future chapters we shall have occasion to return to some of them.

CHAPTER 3

Jesus Christ as Prophet

We have spoken about Jesus being sent by the Father, and of his seemingly deep awareness of this fact. However, we must go further and ask ourselves, in what way did the early Church think of him as being sent, how did the first disciples come to an understanding of his mission? A careful study of the New Testament brings out the fact that no one category of people, no one title, available at that time, adequately describes him or his mission. He surpasses all the categories, all the titles; he is more than any one of them or even all of them put together. However, each one of them helps us to enter more deeply into the mystery of Christ and what he was sent to do,[1] a mystery that carries us right into the heart of the Godhead. That is why it is necessary to look deeply at the different titles that the New Testament gives to Jesus, because

---

[1]We might recall here the words of Karl Rahner: "There is one point which the dogmatic theologian must again and again make clear to himself on the basis of his own principles and data. It is that however true it may be that according to these dogmatic principles Jesus constitutes a unique reality in saving history such that he must not be placed on the same level as any other prophet, religious personality or inspiring leader, still it is also true that he must be fitted organically into a basic conception of saving history as a whole, even though in fitting him in this way we only realize his position at the supreme point of saving history viewed precisely in this way as a totality after we have achieved the *a*

53

they all point to and throw light on that Mystery of mysteries that is God. Some of them came from the historic Jesus himself. Others came from the ambient of the early Church, either in Palestine or in the Gentile world. All of them, however, were seen as being capable of capturing something of the mystery of this Jesus of Nazareth who was perceived in faith as being the Son of God and the Savior of the world.

There are good reasons for saying that the category of "prophet" as it was understood during the lifetime of Jesus was one of the earliest invoked in an attempt to express the significance of Jesus, and it is even implied that it was used by the historical Jesus himself to help explain his mission. The understanding of Jesus as "prophet" is found in a very special way in the Gospel according to Luke, but not exclusively so.

First, it was within this category that the people of his time tended to place him. For example in Mark's Gospel we read:

> King Herod heard of it; for Jesus' name had become known. Some were saying, "John the baptizer has been raised from the dead; and for this reason these powers are at work in him." But others said, "It is Elijah." And others said, "It is a prophet, like one of the prophets of old" (6:14-15).

This is repeated later on:

> Jesus went on with his disciples to the villages of Caesarea Phillippi; and on the way he asked his disciples, "Who do people say that I am?" And they answered him, "John the Baptist; and others, Elijah; and still others, one of the prophets" (8:27-28).

---

posteriori experience of Jesus. He does indeed constitute the supreme point of saving history, unique and unsurpassable, but he is this precisely within this saving history itself. We are presenting the uniqueness of Jesus in a false light if we regard him merely as the Son of God, setting him in this sense over against men as though initially these had nothing to do with God, or when we view him simply as a messenger from the other world of the divine, entering a world which again has nothing to do with God." "The Position of Christology in the Church Between Exegesis and Dogmatics" in *Theological Investigations* XI (New York: Seabury, 1974, 199–200).

Likewise, after the raising to life of the widow's son at Na'in, we read:

> Fear seized all of them; and they glorified God, saying, "A great prophet has arisen among us!" and, "God has looked favorably on His people!" (Luke 7:16).

Even the Pharisees wondered if he were perchance the long awaited prophet, despite the fact that he did not conform to their idea of what a prophet should be and how he should behave:

> Now when the Pharisee who had invited him saw it, he said to himself, "If this man were a prophet, he would have known who and what kind of woman this is who is touching him—that she is a sinner" (Luke 7:39).

Even John's Gospel bears witness to the ordinary people's tendency to interpret Jesus in terms of messianic prophethood (even though they misunderstood its true nature):

> When the people saw the sign that he had done, they began to say, "This is indeed the prophet who is to come into the world" (John 6:14).

Second, it was not just the crowd, or people from outside who tended to see him as a prophet, but his most intimate circle, his own disciples, recipients of special instruction, also saw him as a prophet:

> He asked them, "What things?" They replied, "The things about Jesus of Nazareth, who was a prophet mighty in deed and word before God and all the people, and how our chief priests and leaders handed him over to be condemned to death, and crucified him" (Luke 24:19-20).

Third, as mentioned earlier, Jesus himself seems to have understood himself within this category, at least to a certain extent. For example, when John the Baptist through his emissaries asks the question: "Are you the one who is to come?" Jesus responds in prophetic language:

> Go and tell John what you hear and see: the blind receive their
> sight, the lame walk, the lepers are cleansed, the deaf hear, the
> dead are raised, and the poor have good news brought to
> them. And blessed is anyone who takes no offense at me (Matt
> 11:4-6).

Some indeed had taken offense at him, and the reply of
Jesus is illuminating:

> "Is not this the carpenter, the son of Mary and brother of
> James and Joses and Judas and Simon, and are not his sisters
> here with us?" And they took offense at him. Then Jesus said
> to them, "Prophets are not without honor, except in their
> hometown, and among their own kin, and in their own
> house" (Mark 6:3-4. Cf. also Luke 4:24 and John 4:44).

In the episode describing his visit to his local synagogue of
Nazareth, we find that he makes prophetic claims for himself:

> When he came to Nazareth, where he had been brought up,
> he went to the synagogue on the sabbath day, as was his custom.
> He stood up to read, and the scroll of the prophet Isaiah was
> given to him, He unrolled the scroll and found the place
> where it was written:
>
>> The Spirit of the Lord is upon me,
>>> because he has anointed me to bring good news to the
>>> poor.
>> He has sent me to proclaim release to the captives
>>> and recovery of sight to the blind,
>>> to let the oppressed go free,
>> to proclaim the year of the Lord's favor.
>
> And he rolled up the scroll, gave it back to the attendant, and
> sat down. The eyes of all in the synagogue were fixed on him.
> Then he began to say to them, "Today this scripture has been
> fulfilled in your hearing" (Luke 4:16-19).

Here we should note the significant phrase: "Today, this
scripture . . . ." for he thereby underlines that he is not just
a prophet, but is the eschatological prophet, the one in whom
Scripture is to be fulfilled.

Luke in particular sees Jesus as fulfilling the promise made long ago to the people of Israel, and recorded in the Book of Deuteronomy, that a prophet like Moses would be sent to them:

> The LORD your God will raise up for you a prophet like me from among your own people; you shall heed such a prophet. This is what you requested of the LORD your God at Horeb on the day of the assembly when you said: "If I hear the voice of the LORD my God any more, or ever again see this great fire, I will die" (18:15-16).

The transfiguration scene where Jesus is depicted as conversing with Moses and Elijah (Matt 17:1-8; Mark 9:2-8; Luke 9:28-36) reinforces this. And like Moses he too was expected to be the liberator of his people:

> And we had hoped that he was the one to redeem Israel (Luke 24:21).

It was in this light also that his death was to be understood:

> Yet today, tomorrow, and the next day I must be on my way, because it is impossible for a prophet to be killed outside of Jerusalem (Luke 13:33).

Peter, on the day of Pentecost makes explicit reference to this:

> You that are Israelites, listen to what I have to say: Jesus of Nazareth, a man attested to you by God with deeds of power, wonders, and signs that God did through him among you, as you yourselves know—this man, handed over to you according to the definite plan and foreknowledge of God, you crucified and killed by the hands of those outside the law (Acts 2:22-23).

We can now ask ourselves the further question: what was the understanding of "prophet" in the tradition of Israel? A prophet was one who spoke on behalf of another, one chosen by God for this purpose, one who was empowered by God to see events in their true significance, to see as it were the events as God sees them, and so to denounce with courage and power all that is opposed to the salvific will of God, all that is opposed to faith, obedience, to justice and to love, and at the same time to promote all that contributes to the realization of Yahweh's plan of salvation, to protect the weak and down-trodden, to be their defense lawyer in cases of injustice and oppression, to console people in times of sorrow and anguish. Even a cursory examination of the great prophets of Israel reveals this pattern.

Even though at the time of Jesus it seemed that the age of the prophets had passed, they were nevertheless revered and cherished in the memory of the people. Furthermore, it was firmly believed that the appearance of a new and definitive prophet would herald the arrival of the messianic age.

In the popular imagination, a prophet at the time of Jesus was understood to be

1. Someone mighty in deeds.
2. Someone mighty in words.
3. Someone full of the Spirit of God.
4. Someone fated to be persecuted and executed.

Mighty in Deeds

There can be no doubt that one of the facts that first impressed the people was that Jesus was mighty in deeds. As already in-dicated it was the spontaneous reaction of the crowd after the raising to life of the dead son of the widow of Na'in. We find the same response from the man who had been cured of his blindness: "So they said again to the blind man, 'What do you say about him? It was your eyes he opened.' He said, 'He is a prophet'" (John 9:17).

And we find the two disciples on the road to Emmaus de-scribing Jesus of Nazareth as "a prophet mighty in deed and word before God and all the people" (Luke 24:19), while Peter on the first Pentecost addresses the inhabitants of Jerusalem, saying: "Jesus of Nazareth, a man attested to you by God with deeds of power, wonders, and signs that God did through him among you, as you yourselves know . . . ." (Acts 2:22).

The "deeds" were therefore first and foremost attestations that God was with his prophet, that his power was active in and through this person. Jesus is recognized as "a great prophet," especially by his power over life and death (cf. Luke 7:11-17, the raising of the widow's son). The people therefore naturally turned to this title to describe what they saw in Jesus: God the Father powerfully active in and through him. The mighty deeds of Jesus are therefore, to use Johannine language, "signs" of God's presence. For the contemporaries of Jesus miracles were not in the first place actions beyond nature, something marvelous, but rather manifestations, indicators of God's presence. For that reason the mighty deeds of Jesus form an integral part of the Gospel story and underline the significance of Jesus for the people: He came to bring life, salvation, to make whole— and he shows this in a clear unambiguous way. Through them the people discover that the Kingdom of God is among them:

> "Are you the one who is to come, or are we to wait for another?" Jesus answered them, "Go and tell John what you hear and see: the blind receive their sight, the lame walk, the lepers are cleansed, the deaf hear, the dead are raised, and the poor have good news brought to them. And blessed is anyone who takes no offense at me" (Matt 11:3-6).

In the not too distant past it was popular to reject the miracle stories of the New Testament as legends invented by the Christians to help explain what Christ meant for them. However, in more recent times there is general acceptance that they are in fact based on historical events of the life of Jesus. As Edward Schillebeeckx puts it:

> There is a historically firm basis for affirming, as the New Testament does, that Jesus acted as both healer and exorcist. The gospels make it clear that a salvation which does not manifest

itself here and now, in respect of concrete, individual human beings, can have nothing in the way of "glad tidings" about it. The dawning of God's rule becomes visible on this earth, within our history, through victory over the "powers of evil." This it is that the miracles of Jesus exemplify. In the struggle with evil Jesus is totally on the side of God. Jesus is a power of goodness that conquers Satan (Mark 3:27 and parallels).[2]

Indeed there are some episodes in the Gospels which would be unintelligible if Jesus were not known as a miracle worker; for example, in Mark's Gospel the accusation of the Pharisees that he cast out devils "by the ruler of the devils" (3:22) or the protest of the apostles that they had found "someone casting out demons in your name" (9:38).

The powerful deeds are at the service of the mission of Jesus, not opportunities for Jesus to show off his power—indeed he consistently refused to use it for that purpose (Matt 4:5-7; Luke 23:6-112; Mark 8:11-13; Matt 12:38-42; Mark 15:31-32). The miracles of Jesus are characterized by a delicate simplicity, totally devoid of showmanship, of the spectacular or extravagant gesture. Rather than stress the event itself, he constantly stresses the importance of faith for a true appreciation of the mighty deeds and a true understanding of their significance. Miracles as such presupposed faith. Faith is the link between God and his power, between God and salvation, and this is as true today as it was in the time of Jesus. Faith was the means of entering into contact with the power of God active in Jesus Christ. For that reason Jesus constantly stresses the importance of believing, having faith, trusting in God, in his presence. Faith is allowing God to break in on one's life, letting God be God for me. One could even describe the work of Jesus as that of communicating God's gift of faith to humanity.

That is his central role as the Missionary, and is the central role of all God's missionaries. To continue to do the mighty

[2]Edward Schillebeeckx, *Jesus. An Experiment in Christology* (New York: Seabury, 1979) 189.

works of Jesus is to continue to show God's love present in the world, a love capable of transforming the universe, of destroying sin and death, and that is the mighty deed of God. Miracles in the life of Jesus were signs of his liberating mission to humanity, signs that what he had come to bring was life, not death; signs of God's desire that all human beings be whole, entire, complete.

Furthermore, the "signs" of Jesus, his "mighty deeds" are not exterior to Jesus, as it were, but point to him, as *the* sign of God's presence. He himself *is* the mighty deed of God, *is* the true, authentic sign of God's presence, without any shade or darkness. For that reason he infinitely surpasses the prophet, is more than a prophet, and as such the term is inadequate. The prophets prior to Jesus had worked miracles, and even the apostles had miracles attributed to them, but what is different in the case of Jesus is that he, and only he, performed miracles in his own name. Right in the opening chapter of Mark's Gospel, Jesus is presented as performing a miracle in his own name:

> A leper came to him begging him, and kneeling he said to him, "If you choose, you can make me clean." Moved with pity, Jesus stretched out his hand and touched him, and said to him, "I do choose. Be made clean!" Immediately the leprosy left him, and he was made clean (1:40-42). (Cf. 2:11, 5:41, etc.)

But just as a drawing of a certain reality can help us to recognize it with security when we encounter it, so the category of "prophet" can help us to recognize the mystery of Jesus when it is revealed to us in the gift of faith.

Mighty in Word

There is no doubt that for the Jews the most salient characteristic of a prophet was his or her word—a word seen as coming not from within the prophet primarily, but from Yahweh. The prophet enunciates the Word of Yahweh. Of the 241 times that the phrase "The word of Yahweh" is found in the Old Testament, no less than 221 refer to a prophetic oracle.[3] The word was central to the prophetic function.

For us in the Western world of the late twentieth century, it is difficult to capture the significance of the word for the people of two thousand years ago. For these latter the word was not just a mere label to attach to some object, a mere vehicle for communicating certain intellectual ideas: it was something powerful in itself, something effective, creative. And this was particularly so when applied to the word of God—the *dabar Yahweh*. It was creative of salvation.

It was the one word of God that brought the world into existence, and this same word that effects the salvation of that world. Creation, revelation and salvation are all to be understood within the one category "word of God." It could draw down blessings on an individual or group, or, through one's rejection of it, draw down a curse. It was a judge that could grant pardon or pass sentence of condemnation. This was particularly true of the prophetic word, for that was perceived as not just the word of a human being, but the word of Yahweh:

> By the word of the Lord the heavens were made,
> and all their host by the breath of his mouth . . . .
> For he spoke, and it came to be;
> he commanded, and it stood firm (Ps 33:6, 9).

Indeed the whole history of Israel was seen as the working out in time of God's word. "Word" was the best way of describing God's revelatory activity, his personal openness to the world, even though this activity was more all-embracing than the actual physical word. Thus, within the prophetic tradition the actions of the prophets as well as their preaching were regarded as the "word of Yahweh." To the prophets God communicated his plan of salvation, and they in turn made it known to the people: Amos puts it like this:

[3]See Gerhard von Rad, *The Message of the Prophets* (New York: Harper and Row, 1967) 66.

> Surely the Lord God does nothing,
> without revealing his secret
> to his servants the prophets (Amos 3:7).

Jesus was seen first of all as fitting into this tradition. Through him God has spoken definitively to the world. All God's former "words" come to their fullness in him:

> Long ago God spoke to our ancestors in many and various ways by the prophets, but in these last days he has spoken to us by a Son, whom he appointed heir of all things, through whom he also created the worlds (Heb 1:1-2).

Referring to the prophetic word of Jesus reminds us immediately of his preaching ministry. His mission was to "proclaim good news," and it is this aspect of his mission that receives the most prominence in the Gospels. His preaching explains his life and his death, his *raison d'etre*. Without his preaching, without his prophetic word, the central event of his earthly existence, the Paschal mystery, would be unintelligible, unapproachable for us. The people were profoundly impressed by the power of his word, and this comes through in the Gospel tradition.

> And when Jesus had finished these sayings, the crowds were astonished at his teaching, for he taught them as one having authority, and not as their scribes (Matt 7:28-29 and parallels).

> They were all amazed, and they kept on asking one another, "What is this? A new teaching—with authority! He commands even the unclean spirits, and they obey him" (Mark 1:27).

> The centurion answered, "Lord I am not worthy to have you come under my roof; but only speak the word, and my servant will be healed" (Matt 8:8).

> That evening they brought to him many who were possessed with demons; and he cast out the spirits with a word, and cured all who were sick (Matt 8:16).

> Jesus said to him, "Go; your son will live." The man believed the word that Jesus spoke to him and started on his way. As he was going down, his slaves met him and told him that his child was alive. So he asked them the hour when he began to recover,

and they said to him, "Yesterday at one in the afternoon the fever left him." The father realized that this was the hour when Jesus had said to him, "Your son will live" (John 4:50-53).

For which is easier, to say, "Your sins are forgiven," or to say, "Stand up and walk"? But so that you may know that the Son of Man has authority on earth to forgive sins—he then said to the paralytic—"Stand up, take your bed and go to your home" (Matt 9:5-6 and parallels).

Joseph Fitzmeyer, in his commentary on Luke 11:29-32 argues that the "sign of Jonah" in its original setting in the ministry of Jesus referred to his preaching as a prophet, and, he says, "as a reference to Jesus' resurrection is scarcely to be attributed to Jesus himself," as is implied in the Matthew parallel of the passage.[4]

The preaching of Jesus as prophet is generally interpreted as reaching its high point in the "Sermon on the Mount" (or "on the plain" as in Luke), regarded as the major "sermon" of Jesus. But here again we discover the aspect of "more than"! Jesus does not introduce his preaching with the time-honored prophetic formula: "The word of God . . . ." but rather states: "But I say to you . . . ."

You have heard that it was said to those of ancient times . . . . But I say to you . . . . (Matt 5:21f.).

He claims for his own words the same response as to the word of God:

Everyone then who hears these words of mine and acts on them will be like a wise man who built his house on rock . . . . (Matt 7:24f.).

---

[4]Fitzmyer writes: "Hence in this Lucan passage one must note: Just as Jonah was a prophet sent from afar to preach repentance to the Ninevites, so too does Jesus appear to this generation . . . He comes from afar in the sense of a heaven-sent prophet like Jonah; but he is something greater than Jonah. His preaching is the only sign that will be given to this generation; indeed, the note of irony is unmistakable, since this sign is already being given." *The Gospel According to Luke* (New York: Doubleday, Anchor Bible) II, 933.

We find the same idea in the parable of the Sower who went out to sow the seed (Matt 13:3-23 and parallels).

Gradually it was borne in on the early Christians as they reflected on the life, death, and resurrection of Jesus, that he was not just the proclaimer of the word of God, but that he himself was the Word, that he himself is God's definitive saving Word directed to the world, that he *is* the Gospel message, the good tidings. And so Jesus has all the characteristics of the words of God—creative, revelatory, salutary—and these in a total, perfect way. In this way the early Church was able to express in a profound manner the relationship between God and Jesus Christ, enabled to apply to Jesus the attributes which they had applied to Yahweh.

This receives its most perfect New Testament expression in the Gospel of John—a Gospel which stands out from the others by virtue of its "high" Christology. This Gospel utilized the Hellenic concept of the *logos*, the "word" to express not only the power or dynamism of God's word in Jesus Christ but also the profound identity between the creative and redemptive word of God. Here we will not go into the full implications of the Johannine *logos*, except to mention that the use of this Hellenistic concept helped to clarify and draw out the implications of the Old Testament concept of the *dabar*, without in any way undermining or destroying the priority of this latter term. The Hellenic is at the service of the Israelite notion, not vice-versa. As Cullmann pointed out, "The Johannine reflection had a quite different beginning point: a concrete event, the life of Jesus."[5]

And he goes on to say:

> The Word of Jesus—the word he preached—plays such an important part in the whole Gospel of John that one can hardly assume the evangelist did not think also of this "word" when in the prologue he identified Jesus himself as the Logos. The supposition that he did so is suggested even more strongly by

---

[5]Oscar Cullmann, *The Christology of the New Testament* (Philadelphia: Westminster, 1959) 265.

the basic Johannine thought that Jesus not only *brings* revelation, but in his person *is* revelation. He brings light, and at the same time he is Light; he bestows life and he is Life; He proclaims truth, and he is Truth. More properly expressed, he brings light, life and truth just because he himself is Light, Life, and Truth. So it is also with the Logos: he brings the word, because he is the Word.[6]

Christ *is* therefore *the* prophet in the most perfect and complete sense, and his mission received from the Father is precisely to proclaim to the world the Father and the Father's plan of salvation. The word of the Father, the "word of the Lord" is, as we have seen, constitutive of prophecy, and because Jesus is in the most profound sense the "word" of the Father, in his whole being and action, in all his words and gestures, then he is the very manifestation, the very epiphany of the Father. From the first moment of the incarnation right up to his glorious ascension into heaven Jesus never ceases to be the Word of the Father, the Word of God. He is the prophet of the Father, the witness *par excellence* of the Father and of his salvific will. Because only he really knows the Father (cf. John 7:29), only he in the strict sense comes from the Father (John 8:42), only he knows the Father's plan of salvation and communicates it to human beings (John 5:19-47), only he, therefore, is the fullness and completion of all prophecy. He is the substantive, definitive Word of the Father, so that after him there is no more, nor can there be more, to be revealed. We will return to this concept again.

Someone Full of the Spirit of God

In the Old Testament it was clear that the prophets were men chosen and guided by the Spirit of God. Samuel, for example, is told: "Then the spirit of the Lord will possess you, and you will be in a prophetic frenzy along with them and be turned into a different person" (1 Sam 10:6).

[6]Idem.

At the anointing of David we read: "Then Samuel took the horn of oil, and anointed him in the presence of his brothers; and the Spirit of the LORD came mightily upon David from that day forward" (1 Sam 16:13).

The prophet Micah tells us:

> But as for me, I am filled with power,
>   with the spirit of the LORD,
>   and with justice and might,
> to declare to Jacob his transgression
>   and to Israel his sin (3:8).

Hosea uses "man of the spirit" as a synonym for "prophet":

> The prophet is a fool,
>   the man of the spirit is mad! (9:7).

Ezechiel tells us: "And when he spoke to me, a spirit entered into me and set me on my feet; and I heard him speaking to me" (2:2; see also 3:12ff.; 8:3; 11:1ff.).

Jesus is the man of the Spirit *par excellence*. This is brought out especially by the evangelist Luke. Over and over again he reminds his readers that all is accomplished by the power of the Spirit. Jesus is conceived by the power of the Spirit: "The Holy Spirit will come upon you, and the power of the Most High will overshadow you; therefore the child to be born will be holy; he will be called Son of God" (1:35).

At his baptism, the Holy Spirit descends upon him, (3:22), and afterwards "full of the Holy Spirit," "he was led by the Spirit in the wilderness" (4:1) and he inaugurates his public life by applying the words of the prophet Isaiah to himself:

> The Spirit of the Lord is upon me,
>   because he has anointed me
>   to bring good news to the poor (4:18).

In this text Luke underlines the intimate relation of the Spirit to the mission of Jesus. It is the Spirit that makes the activity of Jesus fruitful. After his fast for forty days in the desert, we are told that "then Jesus, filled with the power of the Spirit, returned to Galilee, and a report about him spread through all the surrounding country" (Luke 4:14).

After the return of the seventy, we read that Jesus "rejoiced in the Holy Spirit" (10:21). The activity of Jesus on earth is dominated totally by the Holy Spirit and for that reason Satan has no power over him, and is unable to distract him from his mission, or to entice him to abandon it in any way (4:2-13). Opposition to the Spirit, Jesus tells us, is the unpardonable sin: "Whoever speaks a word against the Son of Man will be forgiven, but whoever speaks against the Holy Spirit will not be forgiven, either in this age or in the age to come" (Matt 12:32; see Luke 12:10; Mark 3:29).

However, once again we realize that Jesus is guided by the Spirit in a new and powerful way, that the presence of the Spirit in him is "more than" the presence of the Spirit in the prophets. In him there is no obstacle to the work of the Spirit, but rather total docility. As his name implies Jesus Christ is indeed the Anointed One of God, anointed in his very being and activity by the Holy Spirit. Luke brings this out in the second part of his work when he writes:

> The kings of the earth took their stand,
> And the rulers have gathered together
>   against the Lord and against his Messiah (Acts 4:26).

It was this all embracing presence of the Spirit of God active in Jesus Christ that led the early disciples to see in him someone more than a prophet, more than a powerful rabbi and preacher. He, like God, can send the Holy Spirit and promises to do so:

> When the Advocate comes, whom I will send to you from the Father, the Spirit of truth who comes from the Father, he will testify on my behalf (John 15:26).

> But you will receive power when the Holy spirit has come upon you; you will be my witnesses in Jerusalem, in all Judea and Samaria, and to the ends of the earth (Acts 1:8).

And this promise is fulfilled on Pentecost, when the first Christians experience salvation through the coming of the Spirit. The Holy Spirit is the Guarantor of the whole process of revelation, the One in whom the whole movement of salvation is brought to completion. At Pentecost the young Church becomes the new body of Christ, animated by the same Spirit, and therefore capacitated to take over and continue his mission, and consequently the power and vitality of the mission of the Church is due to the power and vitality of the Spirit. Mission and the Holy Spirit cannot be separated just as mission and Christ cannot be separated. In John's Gospel there is, I feel, a beautiful reference to this. Jesus dies on the cross, and the evangelist reports it in the words: "When Jesus had received the wine, he said, 'It is finished.' Then he bowed his head and gave up his spirit" (19:30).

In this text the phrase that is translated by "gave up his spirit" is *paradoken to pneuma* (*tradidit spiritum*), and this could be equally translated as "he handed on the spirit." I think therefore that John is giving here a veiled reference to the fact that on leaving this world Jesus passes on his Spirit to those who stand at the foot of the cross, passes on his mission and the power to realize it.

It is through the power of the Spirit that the individual or community is enabled to confess Christ: "By this you know the Spirit of God: every spirit that confesses that Jesus Christ has come in the flesh is from God, and every spirit that does not confess Jesus is not from God" (1 John 4:2-3).

In the New Testament it becomes abundantly clear that the event of Christ is inseparably bound to the event of the Spirit and it is upon these two events that the whole plan of salvation revolves. The Incarnation must never be separated from Pentecost.

Someone Fated to Be Persecuted and Executed

In Matthew's Gospel we read the words put on the lips of Jesus: "Jerusalem, Jerusalem, the city that kills the prophets and stones those who are sent to you!" (23:37).

In the minds of the Jews suffering and eventually death were part and parcel of the fate of the prophets. So often throughout their history they had seen the prophets rejected and despised by the leaders of the people. It was probably this awareness of the prophetic nature of his mission that gave Jesus his deep insight into the inevitability of his own death. In that same chapter 23 of Matthew, we hear the Lord's powerful diatribe against the Scribes and Pharisees, and in the course of which he says:

> Woe to you, scribes and Pharisees, hypocrites! For you build the tombs of the prophets and decorate the graves of the righteous, and you say, "If we had lived in the days of our ancestors, we would not have taken part with them in shedding the blood of the prophets." Thus you testify against yourselves that you are descendants of those who murdered the prophets. Fill up, then, the measure of your ancestors (13:29-32).

It is this consciousness of being a prophet that makes him accept the fact that he must enter into Jerusalem, despite his awareness that there his life is at risk: "Yet today, tomorrow, and the next day I must be on my way, because it is impossible for a prophet to be killed outside of Jerusalem" (Luke 13:33).

It was probably this aspect that caused the early Church to have recourse to the title prophet in order to try and explain or at least come to terms with the terrible scandal of the Cross. Because he *was the* prophet, he must die. "But what God foretold by the mouths of all the prophets, that his Christ should suffer, he thus fulfilled" (Acts 3:18). Indeed, he himself had prophesied his own violent end. He was the supreme prophet of his own mission.

Here, it is notable the combination of two titles, that of prophet and that of Son of Man. As so often throughout the New Testament, the titles intertwine and mutually enlighten. In combining the two ideas of the eschatological prophet and the Suffering Servant of Yahweh, we enter into a deeper understanding of his mission. For his death is not something extrinsic to his mission but rather is an intimate part of it.

> For the Son of man came not to be served but to serve, and
> to give his life a ransom for many (Mark 10:45).

> For as the lightning flashes and lights up the sky from one
> side to the other, so will the Son of Man be in his day. But
> first he must endure much suffering and be rejected by this
> generation (Luke 17:24-25).

> Then he began to teach them that the Son of Man must un-
> dergo great suffering, and be rejected by the elders, the chief
> priests, and the scribes, and be killed, and after three days rise
> again (Mark 8:31).

> As they were gathering in Galilee, Jesus said to them, "The
> Son of Man is going to be betrayed into human hands, and
> they will kill him, and on the third day he will be raised." And
> they were greatly distressed (Matt 17:22-23).

Even in the midst of his power and acceptance by the
people, he alerted them to the suffering that awaited him:

> While everyone was amazed at all that he was doing, he said
> to his disciples, "Let these words sink into your ears: The Son
> of Man is going to be betrayed into human hands." But they
> did not understand this saying; its meaning was concealed
> from them, so that they could not perceive it. And they were
> afraid to ask him about this saying (Luke 9:43-44).

So, once again we discover that Jesus is not just *a* prophet,
or even *the* prophet, but rather he is *more than* a prophet. The
category describes him but not adequately. He surpasses it.
The inadequacy of the title to fully describe Jesus was appre-
ciated by the early Church,[7] but at the same time, through it we
discover certain aspects of his mission, that for which he was
sent into the world. We can better appreciate his freedom before
the Law. Like the prophets of old, Jesus too is aware that the
source of his teaching is God himself, that he is full of God's
Spirit, and so is not bound by any mere man-made laws or

[7]See, for example, Joseph A. Fitzmyer, *The Gospel According to Luke*
(New York: Doubleday, Anchor Bible, 1981) I.213–5.

customs. Like the ancient prophets he too must proclaim the word of God, reveal God's mighty plan of salvation in word and deed, call the people to fidelity to the covenant, denounce hypocrisy and promote Godliness—that is charity. But unlike them, he not only proclaims and reveals, he brings about, effects that which he proclaims and reveals. He not only utters the Word of God, he *is* the Word of God; he *is* God's mighty plan of salvation; he *is* humanity's fidelity to the covenant. He is not just the prophet of the past, present, and future of the history of salvation, but the very fulfillment of that history.

The prophet's mantle has passed to the Church. Like him she too must be mighty in word and deed, strong and fearless in proclaiming the Good News of the Kingdom of God, and, through the power of the Spirit of the Risen Lord in her, making that Kingdom a reality in the world in which she lives. And again like him she must expect and indeed embrace the fate that this mission entails. Suffering and the cross will not be far from her. This brings us to a closer look at the Kingdom of which Jesus was the prophet.

CHAPTER 4

Jesus and the Kingdom

After our brief look at Jesus as Prophet, it is natural for us to move on to a consideration of Jesus as the Prophet of the Kingdom. According to the Gospel of Matthew, Jesus opens his public life of preaching with the words: "Repent, for the Kingdom of heaven has come near" (4:17). Matthew, following the rabbinical usage, tends to use the Semitic circumlocution "Kingdom of *heaven*" out of a sense of reverence, while Mark and Luke favor the phrase, "Kingdom of *God*." The two expressions are equivalent. Mark tells us: "Now after John was arrested, Jesus came to Galilee, preaching the good news of God, and saying, 'The time is fulfilled, and the Kingdom of God has come near; repent and believe in the good news'" (1:14-15). It should be noted that Jesus as prophet of the Kingdom shows himself to be different from all the other prophets. The prophets prior to Jesus had proclaimed a kingdom that was to come; Jesus comes offering the Kingdom as a present reality: "But if it is by the Spirit of God that I cast out demons, then the kingdom of God has come to you" (Matt 12:28; also Luke 11:20, 17:21).

There is no doubt that the phrase "Kingdom of God" goes right back to the historical Jesus himself, and indeed it can be counted among the *ipsissima verba Jesu*.[1] It was not a phrase that was current in the Judaism of his time, and in the

---

[1]This would seem to be proven by the fact that it conforms to the following criteria: (1) the criterion of discontinuity: the phrase was not

Old Testament, the phrase "kingdom of God" is only found once, in Wisdom 10:10, nor was it current in the primitive Church. However, the idea of God being king of Israel was very deep in the consciousness of his people, so that the phrase, "Kingdom of God," while not being in vogue at the time of Jesus, was one to which Jesus could have presumed a certain responsiveness on the part of his audience, due to the kingship theme found in the Old Testament.[2]

In the so-called Song of Moses, (Exod 15:1-18) Yahweh is presented as the King of Israel, who "will reign for ever and ever" (v. 18). The hymn presents him as the one who rules Israel, who has formed Israel into a people, who protects Israel and saves his people from their enemies. He is the warrior King. This awareness in Israel of Yahweh as King explains their reluctance to elect an earthly king. In the early days, when this idea began to surface, Gideon tells them: "I will not rule over you, and my son will not rule over you; the Lord will rule over you" (Judg 8:23). In the end, and with Yahweh's express approval and approbation, a king is chosen but one whose subordination to Yahweh must always be kept in mind. David is presented as the ideal King of Israel, not because of his moral goodness—and the Bible does not gloss over his lapses in that area!—nor even because of his ability to rule, but rather because of his submission to Yahweh, his recognition of his absolutely subordinate role to Yahweh. This is what constituted him the favorite king of Israel.

God is the Lord of creation, and the only one with the absolute right to be called "King." It is not surprising then that Jesus should utilize such a phrase as "Kingdom of God,"

---

common in the Jewish world at that time, nor was it common in the primitive Church; (2) the criterion of multiple attestation, for we find it in at least five independent literary traditions—that of Mark, the "Q" tradition, the tradition proper to Matthew, that proper to Luke, and that proper to John; (3) the criterion of coherence: it fits in admirably with proven historical data about the life and times of Jesus of Nazareth.

[2]For a good treatment of the theme as found in the Old Testament and later Judaism, see Rudolf Schnackenburg, *God's Rule and Kingdom* (New York, 1963) 11–75.

and right through his public life, the Kingdom formed the central motif of all his preaching, as is witnessed to by the different layers of tradition. Rudolf Schnackenburg says, referring to the preaching of Jesus, "Everything is subordinated to the proclamation of the *basileia* and related to the mystery of his own person."[3] Jesus is the *Messiah,* the anointed one whose mission is to proclaim the coming of God's reign foretold by Isaiah. In Mark alone we find it 13 times, in the source common to Matthew and Luke, 9 times, in Matthew alone 27 times, and in Luke alone 12 times. In the whole New Testament the term Kingdom, *basileia,* is found no less than 162 times. Furthermore, not only do we find it in his preaching, but also in his attitudes and actions. That is why one can say that Jesus is the prophet of the Kingdom, but a very special prophet in that he makes present what he preaches; he not only proclaims the Kingdom of God, he himself, in his own person, in his life, inaugurates it and makes it present. In a very special way the Good News is the Kingdom. As Jesus presents it, the Kingdom of God is nothing less than God himself sharing in our human condition, entering into the heart of our history, identifying himself in our existence in the most profound and intimate manner possible. This impressed itself so profoundly on Origen that he refers to Christ as the *autobasileia:* "And as he is himself wisdom itself and justice itself and truth itself, so perhaps he is also himself the *kingdom itself.*"[4]

Nowhere in the Gospels does Jesus define what exactly he means by the Kingdom of God, but a close scrutiny of his use of the phrase underlines that it referred to God's way of dealing with the world. Edward Schillebeeckx puts it like this: "What Jesus intends by it is a process, a course of events, whereby God begins to govern or to act as king or Lord, an action, therefore, by which God manifests his being God in the world of men."[5]

[3]Ibid. 79.

[4]*Or. Matt. 14.7.* Quoted by Benedict T. Viviano in *The Kingdom of God in History* (Wilmington: Glazier, 1988) 40.

[5]Edward Schillebeeckx, *Jesus. An Experiment in Christology* (New York: Seabury, 1979) 141.

It was the natural framework, therefore, within which his whole life and preaching are to be understood. The fact that the Kingdom of God can be understood from two perspectives made it ideal to express the special reality of Jesus as true God and true man. For the Kingdom of God can be viewed from God's point of view: he is its Ruler; or it can be viewed from man's standpoint: man as the subject of the rule. Jesus brings a new understanding to both of these aspects. Norman Perrin has argued persuasively and insightfully that "Kingdom of God" is a *symbol,* rather than a *concept.*[6] Keeping this point in mind I believe is helpful towards achieving a better understanding of Jesus' constant reference to the Kingdom, and enables us to see in this, for us, somewhat mysterious phrase, a shorthand reference to all that his mission signifies, all that his message contains.

From one point of view it sums up the whole plan of salvation, and we see the Kingdom of God gradually, progressively manifesting itself in history, until it achieves its perfect and absolute center in Jesus Christ.[7]

Seeing the Kingdom as a symbol also helps us to understand the constant mixing of tenses—particularly present and future—which we find in Jesus' preaching. For Jesus time is not only chronological, an external measure, not only *chronos,* but is also "time for" something, it is *kairos,*[8]

---

[6]Norman Perrin, *Jesus and the Language of the Kingdom* (Philadelphia: Fortress, 1976) 197. He writes: "Once it was seen as a symbol such unanswerable questions as whether it was present or future, or both, in the message of Jesus could be seen to be false questions, and one could begin to ask the true questions. The questions that should be asked, in my view, are questions as to what kind of symbol Kingdom of God is in the message of Jesus, and what does it evoke or represent."

[7]Paul Tillich, in his *Systematic Theology,* vol. III (Chicago: University of Chicago Press, 1963) has some very interesting insights in this regard. See particularly pp. 297–420.

[8]The late John A.T. Robinson, in his *In the End God* (Harper and Row, 1968) expresses the difference between *chronos* and *kairos* as follows: "The usual word for "time" in secular Greek is *chronos.* In the Biblical writings, the normal term is *kairos.* It is normal, not merely in the sense that it is more common, but in the sense that it represents the norm or proper standpoint from which time is to be understood. *Kairos* is time

the moment of opportunity, time for embracing the Kingdom, entering into it, inserting oneself into the final era of God's plan of salvation.[9] Keeping in mind the distinction between *kairos* and *chronos,* we are also reminded that the time of the Kingdom is primarily the time of opportunity for us. The "coming of the Kingdom" applies to us rather than to God. As Cyprian of Carthage pointed out in the third century:

> Surely there cannot be a time when God does not reign? What has always existed with him and will never cease to exist could never have a beginning. It is for the coming of our kingdom, then, that we are asking, that kingdom which was promised to us by God and acquired by the blood of Christ poured out in his passion.[10]

For that reason the Kingdom of God as proclaimed by Jesus is something that has profound implications for each and every person and for the whole Church. It has repercussions that are spiritual and material, political and social, temporal and eternal. Throughout the history of Christianity this whole range of application of the teaching of the Kingdom has often been neglected, and we find one aspect being exalted at the expense of others. In our century we have seen a rediscovery of

---

considered in relation to personal action, determined by reference to ends to be achieved in it. *Chronos* is time abstracted from such a relation, time, as it were, that ticks on objectively and impersonally, whether anything is happening or not. It is time measured by the chronometer not by purpose, momentary rather than momentous" (56–57). In passing, we can also mention that Robinson points out that when we move from the *kairos* conception to the *chronos* conception, we tend to move from a prophetic outlook to an apocalyptic outlook (see p. 58). I think this is relevant for our understanding of Jesus' proclamation of the Kingdom, which is primarily prophetic, although the apocalyptic element is not entirely absent.

[9]See Edward Schillebeeckx, *Christ: The Experience of Jesus as Lord* (New York: Crossroad, 1980) 543.

[10]*De orat. dom. 13,* quoted by Benedict T. Viviano, *The Kingdom of God in History,* 37.

the centrality of the Kingdom[11] idea not only in the mission of Christ but also in the mission of the Church.

Moreover, historically the idea of the Kingdom of God and the understanding of what it signifies have not always been happy. Very often it has been used to legitimate the established order. Indeed, almost from the time of Constantine onwards there was a certain tendency to identify the Kingdom with the Constantinian rule, and later with the Carolingian Holy Roman Empire. And, contrariwise, it has also been used to subvert this same established order, paradoxical as that may seem. Not a few revolutionary movements have found their inspiration in the idea of the Kingdom of God—for example that of Thomas Muentzer in Germany in the early part of the sixteenth century. At other times there was a tendency to identify the Kingdom of God here on earth with the Church.[12] The Church is not the Kingdom, but is in the service of the Kingdom and strives to facilitate the coming of the Kingdom.[13]

John A. T. Robinson has written in this regard:

> Such is the Biblical perspective, in which the Church is called to be the avant-garde of the Kingdom, the eschatological community whose "transcendent" life is to serve as the sign, within this age or saeculum (that is to say, in the midst of the secular), of the open future of man and of all creation's destiny.[14]

[11]The rediscovery of the Kingdom as a central idea is due mainly to such people as Schleiermacher, Rittschel, Johannes Weiss and Albert Schweitzer. For a discussion of their contribution, see Norman Perrin, *The Kingdom of God in the Teaching of Jesus* (Philadelphia: Westminster, 1963).

[12]The influence of Augustine and his *City of God* is powerful in this respect. Augustine said that there is a partial identification of the Church with the Kingdom, and this partial identification was, particularly in the Middle Ages, often applied to the Church without the nuances that Augustine himself gave it. Because of that the simple identification of the Church and the Kingdom has been commonplace in the Catholic Church right up to recent times.

[13]For a short review of the whole history of the idea up to modern times see, Benedict T. Viviano, *The Kingdom of God in History.*

[14]John A. T. Robinson, *In the End God*, 14.

The idea of "Kingdom" is not very congenial to our modern democratic ears, yet an understanding of it is vital for an understanding of the Gospel. Indeed, a rediscovery of the notion of the Kingdom of God and all that it signified for Jesus is essential for a renewal of the proclamation of the Gospel.

As indicated above, the word "Kingdom" can be understood in two ways. In the first place it carries the idea of God's *rule* or *sovereignty*. In this sense the Kingdom of God connotes the rule of God over humanity. In Israel, when the king, the anointed of Yahweh, and the people whom he represented forgot their utter dependence on Yahweh, when they rejected his rule, rebelled against him, then retribution and reproof followed. Yahweh had made a treaty with this people, entered into a covenant with them, that he would be their God and they would be his people. Fidelity to this covenant would be their salvation, understood not just in a spiritual, but also in a political manner. Salvation had for the Israelites of old a primarily social connotation, even if the idea of individual salvation was not entirely foreign to them. This social connotation of the phrase must not be forgotten. Too often in the recent history of Christianity, the "Kingdom of God" has been identified with the sanctifying grace in the individual soul,[15] to the detriment of the social implications of the Gospel message. This latter aspect of the Kingdom has been emphasized by modern theologians and exegetes, people like Paul Tillich, Reinhold Niebuhr, Hans Küng, Edward Schillebeeckx, and by the liberation theologians.

Second, the idea carries the connotation of the realm of God's rule, that which belongs to him, is subject to him, that over which he is the Lord. In this sense our thoughts are oriented to the end time, when God will be "all in all." Obviously the two are intimately connected and should not be separated.[16]

[15]See, for example, Louis Perroy, *El Reino de los Cielos* (Bibloa: Desclée de Brouwer, 1958) 74.

[16]In this respect Edward Schillebeeckx writes: "God's 'lordship' or rule and the kingdom of God are two aspects of what the New Testament contains within the single concept *basileia tou Theou*. Mark and Luke speak of the *basileia*, the kingly rule, of God. Peculiar to

So when Jesus used the phrase "Kingdom of God," it would carry the notion for his listeners of God's rule, God's realm, and the coming of the Kingdom would connote the coming of judgment, the exercise of justice in the sense that God would vindicate his people and bring them salvation. Jesus therefore would see no need to explain the fundamental image, but at the same time he would purify it without changing its root meaning. It would still refer to the rule of God, to the realm of God, but he would make it clear that this rule of God is different from what was spontaneously understood by the people, a rule that has to do with presence, rather than external laws.

Through his actions and his preaching, through his very life and death Jesus shows in what the rule/presence of God consists, so that in him the lordship of God is manifested and draws close to humanity. In contemplating Jesus Christ we contemplate God's rule being made manifest before the world, we contemplate the Kingdom. In him the Kingdom of God takes flesh. It is no longer embodied in ideas and concepts, but is embodied in the life, death and resurrection of Jesus Christ. The supreme revelation of what is meant by the "Kingdom of God" takes place on the Cross, and it is here that the deepest

---

Matthew is 'the kingdom of heaven,' where 'heaven' is the late Jewish abstract way of denoting God. *Basileia tou Theou* is the kingdom of God, the rule of God as Lord, the realm of God. It does not denote some area of sovereignty above and beyond this world, where God is supposed to reside and to reign. What Jesus intends by it is a process, a course of events, whereby God begins to govern or to act as God in the world of men. Thus God's lordship or dominion is the divine power itself in its saving activity within our history, but at the same time the final, eschatological state of affairs that brings to an end the evil world, dominated by the forces of calamity and woe, and initiates the new world in which God 'appears to full advantage'; 'your kingdom come' (Mt. 6:10). God's rule and the kingdom of God are thus two aspects of one and the same thing. God's dominion points to the dynamic, here-and-now character of God's exercise of control; the kingdom of God refers more to the definitive state of 'final good' to which God's saving activity is directed. Thus present and future are essentially interrelated." *Jesus. An Experiment in Christology*, 141.

meaning of Jesus as the *Messiah* becomes clear, and he becomes the *Christ*.[17] In the Fourth Gospel, the climax of the trial is presented precisely in terms of Jesus as the messianic King. With typical Johannine irony, it is Pilate, the representative of the Roman Emperor, who presents Jesus at the climax of his trial to the Jews with the phrase: "Behold your king!" To the faithless it was a mockery, an insult, but to the eyes of faith the crown of thorns that he wears is indeed a true crown of royalty, the scepter that he holds in his hands is a true scepter of power— the power that comes from total and complete obedience to his Father, for his life of utter service.[18] And the inscription that is placed over the Cross emphasizes the point: "Jesus of Nazareth, the King of the Jews," and what has been written remains written for all time. "It is therefore certain, for all men and for all time, that Jesus is the King of the Jews. Despite their refusal, the royal sovereignty of Christ is definitely established and proclaimed on the cross."[19]

Jesus was ever profoundly aware of the absolute sovereignty, absolute lordship of God, a lordship that always remains supreme, that must always be recognized and accepted. He was God's slave, and God's slave only. It was this that gave him his supreme freedom. Nothing or nobody, neither his family nor friends, neither the tradition nor the laws of his people, not even his own desires and fears, would be allowed to come between God and his lordship. It is always a case of "not my will, but yours be done." To pray for the coming of

[17]While *Messiah* and *Christ* both mean *Anointed One*, *Messiah* carries the nuance of "the Anointed One of the Kingdom," and *Christ* carries the nuance of "the Anointed One of the Cross." This is particularly clear in Mark's Gospel and helps us to understand the shift within the early Church from the preaching of the Kingdom by Jesus, to the preaching of the crucified Lord by the Church. See Robert A. Guelich, "The 'Christ' of the Gospel: A Lesson from Mark's Christology," in Marguerite Schuster and Richard Mueller, Eds. *Portraits of Christology* (Grand Rapids: Zondervan, 1991) 3–17.

[18]For a scriptural analysis of this passage in John's Gospel, see Ignace De La Potterie, *The Hour of Jesus* (New York: Alba House, 1989) 82–6.

[19]Idem. 97.

God's kingdom, is to pray that his "will be done on earth as it is in heaven."

However, as I have already mentioned, Jesus reveals that this lordship is very different from the usual connotation of lordship here on earth, for the lordship of God is primarily a lordship of love, of mercy, of compassion, of forgiveness, not one of domination, or arrogance. The lordship of God our heavenly Father has nothing to do with male domination or patriarchy in the modern sense of the term, but rather the recognition that God is the source of all good, all that is beautiful, all that is true, all that is loving. The fact that Jesus dares to call God "Abba," dares to call the Almighty, eternal, omnipotent God with the familiar name of "Dad," something that no Jew of his day would have even contemplated doing—underlines that the lordship of God is not a lordship that engenders servile fear, but on the contrary, one that engenders love, trust, confidence, gratitude. For one of the most profound convictions of Jesus Christ as he is portrayed in the Gospels is that God loves all humanity with an all-embracing saving love. This is the core of his Gospel, the core of the Good News, the core of the message he came on earth to proclaim.

It is above all in the parables that Jesus proclaims this truth. As Joachim Jeremias has pointed out:[20] "All Jesus' parables compel his hearers to define their attitude towards his person and mission, for they are all full of 'the secret of the kingdom of God' (Mark 4:11)—that is to say, the certainty that the messianic age is dawning." Norman Perrin expresses the same point as follows:

> The Kingdom of God is the ultimate referent of all the parables of Jesus, and many of them must have been delivered in a form which began with "The kingdom of God is like . . . ." or "It is the case with the Kingdom of God as with . . . ." Such forms have multiple attestation in the Gospel tradition and they would have been wholly appropriate to the historical

[20]In *Rediscovering the Parables* (New York: Scribner's, 1966) 181.

message of Jesus. I need not labor this point; today no scholar doubts it.[21]

The parables, unlike allegories, are usually taken from the normal circumstances of everyday life and as such would have been easily understood by their hearers—at least superficially. And yet so often they contain a strange twist, an unusual out-of-character aspect, sometimes a strange or even shocking punchline. Due to this peculiarity they provoke in us a response to the message of Jesus. Before them one cannot remain neutral. They demand from their hearers a response, a decision, a change in one's way of seeing life, seeing relationships—whether with God, with others, or with oneself. The parables, like the Sermon on the Mount, turn upside down our worldly criteria of judging, relating, evaluating in our world. We discover that it is the rights of others, not our own rights, that must constitute the norm of justice, of righteousness. Like Jesus himself the parables bring home to us how different from ours is God's way of acting, God's way of relating, God's way of forgiving. In and through the parables we discover with wonder and joy God's way of dealing with humanity. For that reason Jesus in his own person is the supreme parable of God. Edward Schillebeeckx has expressed this well:

> Jesus Himself—his person, his stories and his actions—is a parable. Therefore the "shock" effect marks the ongoing sequence of his life. The Marcan gospel saw this very clearly. It brings together (between 2:1 and 3:5) five disconcerting stories, scattered actions of Jesus that oblige those around him to adopt a position towards him; the healing of a paralysed man (whose sin he forgives) (2:1-12)—a meal that Jesus has with tax collectors, people who gathered in monies and revenues for the Romans (2:13-17)—Jesus' defence of his disciples for not fasting when Jesus is with them (2:18-22)—the justification by Jesus of his disciples' behavior when they deliberately pluck ears of corn on the sabbath day (2:23-28)—and lastly,

[21]Norman Perrin, *Jesus and the Language of the Kingdom*, 55.

by way of climax, how Jesus himself heals on the sabbath the withered hand of a man in despair (3:1-5).[22]

In and through the parables we discover the fundamental cause of rejoicing when one accepts in faith the Good News. The coming of God's kingdom is the coming of salvation to all who accept the message in faith, hope, and love. This is why it is a pearl of great price (Matt 13:45f) worthy of giving up all that one possesses in order to attain it. It is the joy of the wedding feast (Mark 2:19), the joy of the shared banquet (Luke 6:21), the joy of finding the lost one (Matt 18:12-14; Luke 15:4-7); the joy of being made whole, made acceptable, made lovable (Matt 8:16, 11:5).

The rule of God is the rule of the shepherd who goes after the lost sheep until he finds it, and having done so carries it back on his shoulders to safety (Luke 15:4-7; Matt 18:12-14); it is the rule of the father who runs somewhat indecorously to embrace the returning son in order to clothe him with the cloak of salvation, (Luke 15:11-32); it is the rule of the housewife who sweeps out the whole house until she finds the lost coin (Luke 15:8-10); it is the rule of the mother hen who gathers the chicks under her wings for protection (Matt 23:37; Luke 13:34); it is the rule of the traveller who, finding a beaten up man on the road, picks him up and cares for him with all the love and care of a doting father or mother (Luke 10:25-37); it is the rule of the physician who tenderly cares for the sick, restores them to full health (Mark 2:17) and even to cure them takes the sickness upon himself (Matt 8:17); it is the rule of the gardener who takes time and patience with the barren fig tree to see if eventually it will bear any fruit (Luke 13:6-9); it is the rule of the landowner who seeks to give employment to those in need of work and to reward them generously for it (Matt 20:1-16); it is the rule that unites, not divides, that is not out to create sects or parties, but rather one great family where the poor, the marginalized, the weak, the sinners, the despised, the pariahs of society can find a home, can find security and peace. It is the rule of one who sits down to eat with sinners, who touches the lepers and heals them, who talks to women despite the strictures of society against it. It is the rule of one who does not take into account the sinful past of anyone, but rather looks to their future with God, who emphasizes not a person's *actuality* but rather his or her *potentiality,* not at what we in fact have done but what we have the potentiality to become, sharers in God's own life.

The Kingdom of God expresses God's justice. So often when we think of justice we are inclined to see it from the point of view of human law: the law's demands must be fulfilled, and true justice consists in the fair, impartial application of the laws of the state. But with God, justice is seen from the point of view of the weak, the oppressed. This aspect is brought out by the psalmist in Psalm 72:

> Give the king your justice, O God,
> and your righteousness to a king's son!
> May he judge your people with righteousness,
> and your poor with justice!
> Let the mountains yield prosperity for the people,
> and the hills, in righteousness!
> May he defend the cause of the poor of the people,
> give deliverance to the needy,
> and crush the oppressor!. . . .
> For he delivers the needy when they call,
> the poor and those who have no helper.
> He has pity on the weak and the needy,
> and saves the lives of the needy.

We find the same idea in Isaiah:

> He shall not judge by what his eyes see,
> or decide by what his ears hear;
> but with righteousness he shall judge the poor,
> and decide with equity for the meek of the earth (11:3-4).

The Kingdom of God, the rule of God, the justice of God is good news for all, but most especially for the "little ones," for the *anawim* of society. For that reason, the poor are blessed, and theirs is the Kingdom, not primarily for anything in themselves, not for their suffering nor their freedom from materialism, not because of their goodness, but because of God's goodness towards them.

In the logic of the Kingdom, it is a case of it coming to us rather than we going to it. We pray "Thy Kingdom come" rather than "Let us go to your Kingdom." The movement is from God to humanity, rather than vice-versa. This has also to be the logic of mission. We must go out to people rather than waiting for them to come to us. In the sending of Christ we once again discover that the priority and initiative belong to him: it was God's movement towards us rather than humanity's movement towards him. It is God, always God, who takes the initiative.

The Kingdom was eagerly awaited by Israel, even though for the most part they completely misunderstood its true nature. They tended to see in it the liberation of Israel from the domination of the Romans. They were right in thinking, however, that the principal role of the Messiah was to usher in this Kingdom, this rule—even though they misunderstood its true nature. Furthermore, the coming of the Kingdom would signify the coming of true, final peace to the world, the true *shalom*, true life.

In the Synoptic Gospels this eschatological aspect of the Kingdom is emphasized. We look forward to the coming of the Kingdom, and our whole life as Christians is colored by this expectation. We look forward to the day when the Lord will rule over the world, when there will be true justice and peace, and no longer will the poor and oppressed be marginalized within human society. For that reason Jesus emphasizes that the fundamental response to the proclamation of the Kingdom is repentance and belief: "The time is fulfilled, and the kingdom of God has come near; repent, and believe in the good news" (Mark 1:15).

Repentance, *metanoia*, is the gate by means of which one enters into the Kingdom of God. This profound change of heart, change of orientation, is such that the focus is concentrated totally on God rather than on oneself or that which is not God. Jesus constantly looked upon humanity from the vantage point of God—and for that reason his proclamation of the Good News springs from God, from God's way of relating to humanity. And the principal motivation that brings about a person's response is also from God, it is the Good News itself rather than the disastrous situation of humanity. John the Baptist had placed all the emphasis on humanity's response to God, the response motivated by the awareness of one's wretchedness. That is what he meant by *metanoia*. But Jesus, while maintaining the same centrality of *metanoia,* saw it from a different viewpoint, from God's viewpoint. The angle of approach was different. In our situation as Christians our response to God should also be motivated not so much by a sense of our own wretchedness, but rather by the overwhelming conviction of God's goodness toward us, God's love for us. It is this that will change our way of acting and thinking, that will rid us of the sins of discrimination, sexism, racism, and all the other barriers between human beings.

For Jesus God always comes first, and it is God's infinite love for humanity that is the Good News and that makes it so imperative for people to respond to it. For Jesus *metanoia* is much more the looking forward to God, to the infinite and wondrous possibilities which he offers to humanity, rather than the looking back with dejection on our own sinful past. Not that the two are mutually exclusive. On the contrary they are mutually inclusive. But it is precisely because God is *love,* because his offer of salvation springs from the very nature of his own interior being, that this Good News is itself the deepest reason for its proclamation. Any true response to love can only be given freely.

This is not to deny in any way the element of judgment that is to be found in the preaching of Jesus. Indeed the proclamation of the Good News of salvation carries with it of necessity the element of judgment. The offer of salvation can be rejected, and because of that God's rule or Kingdom signifies a judgment on humanity, one that humanity cannot avoid. Jesus was deeply aware of this aspect and so over and over again he calls humanity to repent, to turn away from sin before it is too late. His announcing of the Good News of salvation is at the same time the call to sinners to be converted, to change their ways: "I have come to call not the righteous but sinners to repentance" (Luke 5:32). The coming of the Kingdom demands discernment on the part of humankind, to recognize the signs of the time (Luke 12:54-56).

The Good News and judgment are two sides of the one coin. Rejection of the Good News, rejection of God's lordship implies that one remains outside the only love that can bring us to our fullness. In accepting God's lordship humanity discovers its own deepest nature. In accepting and acknowledging the Creator we find our creaturehood, the origin of our being, the only well-spring from which we can have life, and have it more abundantly.

Jesus constantly reminds us that we are entrusted with the knowledge of revelation, with the knowledge of his will, and that one day we will have to render an account of that steward-ship (Matt 24:45-51, Luke 12:42-46). We must be "faithful and wise servants," ever ready to utilize the talents that have been given to us (Matt 25:14-30; Luke 12:35-48). And we are reminded that it is not just enough to know the will of God but we must do it (Luke 12:47-48). Jesus instructed his followers that they were to be "the salt of the earth" but alerted them to the danger of becoming "saltless" (Matt 5:13; Luke 14:34). God calls and patiently waits for our response, but now is the acceptable time to give that response, not when it is too late, when the doors of the wedding feast are closed (the parable of the ten maidens—Matt 25:1-12). We cannot reject the invitation to the messianic banquet with impunity. If one rejects it, then that person excludes himself or herself from it. We are reminded of the parable of the debtor or that of the unjust steward—we must straighten things out before it is too late. We must be on the watch, (Mark 13:35), our lamps ready for the journey (Luke 12:35) with our wedding garment on (Matt 22:11-13).

Thus does Jesus bring out in practical terms what it means to enter into the Kingdom of God: it means letting our lives be ruled by the standards of God, our hearts and our minds molded by the heart and mind of God as revealed in Jesus Christ. His mission was to proclaim the Kingdom of God to humanity, to issue the invitation to all humanity to enter into that realm, place itself under that rulership. But it was not simply a mission of proclamation—he himself was to incarnate the rule of God, incarnate in his very being what it means to exercise the rule of God and what it means to live under that rule, to reveal to us how God rules and how we respond to it. God's rule is a rule of love and compassion, and humanity responds to it by obedience. "My food is to do the will of him who sent me" (John 4:34). "Not what I want but what you want" (Matt 26:39), an obedience that springs not from servile fear but from the profound conviction of God's love, from taking God's word seriously, from faith.

This is the Kingdom which Jesus announces, the Kingdom into which all are invited. And what comes out clearly is that the Kingdom, the rule of God, has come in his own person. And this is the fundamental reason why the early Church did not continue to proclaim the coming of the Kingdom as Jesus had done, but rather the Church proclaimed Jesus Christ. The Proclaimer did indeed become the Proclaimed:[23] "But if it is by the Spirit of God that I cast out demons, then the Kingdom of God has come to you" (Matt 12:28).

In him the promises made to Israel are fulfilled. In him the rule of God enters the world. He is now the lawmaker, who rules with authority, the authority of God. "You have heard that it was said . . . But I say to you" (Matt 5:21-22). Jesus not only proclaims the Good News of the Kingdom; he *is* the

---

[23]See Rudolf Bultmann, *Theology in the New Testament* (New York: Scribner's, 1951, vol. 1): "As the synoptic tradition shows, the earliest Church resumed the message of Jesus and through its preaching passed it on. So far as it did only that, Jesus was to it a teacher and prophet. But Jesus was more than that to the Church: He was also the Messiah; hence that Church also proclaimed him, himself—and that is the essential thing to see. He who formerly had been the bearer of the message was drawn into it and became its essential content. The proclaimer became the proclaimed . . . ." (33).

Good News of the Kingdom. The coming of the Kingdom is so joined to his person, that to reject him is to reject the Kingdom of God in our lives, to accept him is to accept God's lordship, God's rule, to enter into God's Kingdom: "Those who are ashamed of me and of my words in this adulterous and sinful generation, of them the Son of man will also be ashamed when he comes in the glory of his Father with the holy angels" (Mark 8:38).

The very fact that he claims for himself the power to forgive sins shows that he understood himself as within the logic of the Kingdom, of the rule of God, the realm of God.

In Jesus we discover the peculiar logic of the Kingdom, in his way of dealing with people, his way of loving, his mercy, forgiveness. Through him we discover the newness of the rule of God, a rule that dictates that we love our enemies, that we control our hearts and our minds, not just our actions, a rule that is open to all, that does not exclude anybody. To submit to this rule demands recognition of one's real poverty, one's real and permanent dependence on God: "Blessed are the poor in spirit, for theirs is the kingdom of heaven."

This likewise underlines that the Kingdom of God is not brought about by the striving of humanity but is a result of God's unbounded goodness, a pure gift arising from the free initiative of God himself—a gift that he communicates to us in Jesus Christ. That is why the Kingdom of God is as mysterious as God himself. It is already present in the world, and yet we must strive to "bring it about," pray that it may come, that it will be accepted, that the whole world will enter into it. Jesus himself made no secret about its mysterious nature:

> Once Jesus was asked by the Pharisees when the kingdom of God was coming, and he answered, "The kingdom of God is not coming with things that can be observed; nor will they say, 'Look, here it is!' or 'There it is!' For, in fact, the kingdom of God is among you" (Luke 17:20-21).

This point reminds us that the mission of evangelization is the mission of *revealing* the Kingdom that is already present, but present in a hidden way, and so there are those who do not see, who are deceived, who think that it is "here" or "there." Evangelization is removing the veil, enabling men and women to enter into the life of the loving, saving God who is present at the heart of history, at the center of human existence.

Because Jesus incarnates the Kingdom of God in his very life, death, and resurrection, it should not surprise us that the early Church should preach the Good News in terms of the life, death, and resurrection of Jesus, rather than in terms of the Kingdom of God. Through the experience of the resurrection they realized that in Jesus Christ, the Kingdom had received its perfect embodiment, its perfect model, both from the point of view of God and from the point of view of man. Pope John Paul II in his encyclical letter *Redemptoris missio* expresses this point in the following words:

> The Kingdom of God is not a concept, a doctrine, or a program subject to free interpretation, but is before all else a person with the face and name of Jesus of Nazareth, the image of the invisible God. If the Kingdom is separated from Jesus, it is no longer the Kingdom of God which He revealed (no. 18).

Taking the Kingdom of God into account is of the utmost importance for the Church in her preaching, and especially for her missionaries. If we are sent to proclaim the Good News of Jesus Christ, then we are to learn from Jesus himself how to do it. The Kingdom must be the *raison d'etre* of his disciples' lives as it was for his. His preaching must be the model of ours, the emphasis which he gave must be the emphasis which we give. The rule of God as proclaimed and exemplified by him must be the rule that we present before others, a rule that unites not divides, a rule that is open to all and prepared to embrace all, a rule that knows the meaning of love and compassion, a rule that does not make exception of persons, a rule that gives a special place to the poor, the weak, the suffering, the marginalized, sinners, a rule that recognizes at all times the absolute rights of God. A vision of the Kingdom must be the dynamic force that lies behind our teaching and preaching of Jesus Christ, a vision of that which still lies ahead and which motivates all our struggle. The apostles perceived their mission as first and foremost the announcing of the Kingdom, promoting its growth in season and out of season:

> And he appointed twelve, whom he also named apostles, to be with him, and to be sent out to proclaim the message, and to have authority to cast out demons (Mark 3:14).

> As you go, proclaim the good news, "the kingdom of heaven has come near" (Matt 10:7).

To adhere to the Kingdom, to enter into it, is at the same time to work for it. The call of the Kingdom is a call to abandon oneself to the Lord and to make his mission one's own.

If we do this then we in our turn are evangelized, and we hear the Good News with rejoicing, with gratitude, with love. We are enabled to enter ever more deeply into God's space, into the special logic of the Kingdom, or as Segundo Galilea calls it, the *mistica* of the Kingdom,[24] so contrary in so many respects to the logic of the world. Over and over again the missionary has to insert himself/herself in this logic of the Kingdom, to resist the pull of the logic of the world, the logic of egoism and selfishness, the logic of sin. This is the *metanoia* to which the missionary is called day by day. Like Jesus the missionary must incarnate the Kingdom and this is possible only through the power of the Spirit of Jesus poured out upon us. The aim of all evangelization is to invite our brothers and sisters to enter with us into the Kingdom in all its fullness. It is interesting that Scripture does not speak so much about the "extension" of God's Kingdom, or the "building up" of God's Kingdom, but rather speaks about "receiving" his Kingdom, or "entering" into his Kingdom, and these two verbs underline the ever present aspect of our own conversion united with our desire to share the Good News with others. We too have to enter into the Kingdom, receive it into our hearts each day, and

---

[24]See Segundo Galilea, *El Reino de Dios y La Liberacion del Hombre* (Colombia: Paulinas, 1992, 3ra ed.) 41.

only if we do so can we invite others to join us. Entry into the Kingdom, reception of the Kingdom, is a gift from God, a gift that is to be shared with others. The Good News can only be truly received when the necessity to share it becomes imperative. When we are captivated by the joy of its goodness, then it overflows to all whom we meet. We long to see it in its perfection.

This last point underlines that the Kingdom is still awaited in its fullness. As so often in any examination of the realities of Christianity we come to this paradox of "already" and "still not yet." Jesus entered into time, and in doing so revealed the horizon of all time—he revealed what is the absolute future of all time. In his own history the history of the world is revealed; in his casting out of devils the ultimate victory over evil is not only foreshadowed, it is already present: "But if it is by the Spirit of God that I cast out demons, then the Kingdom of God has come to you" (Matt 12:28).

In Jesus we have been rescued

> from the power of darkness and transferred [us] into the kingdom of his beloved Son in whom we have redemption, the forgiveness of sins (Col 1:13).

for

> if anyone is in Christ, there is a new creation; everything old has passed away; see, everything has become new (2 Cor 5:17).

At the same time we are all too painfully aware that the struggle goes on, sin abounds, death is everywhere to be found. What are we to say in this situation? How are we to proclaim to the world that the Kingdom of God has come in Jesus Christ and at the same time admit the obvious reality all about us?

To answer this we have to go back again to Christ—who he is and what he is. In him God entered directly into the historical process. In him the Kingdom—Christ himself—had arrived. The final consummation, the end time, was in him already perceptible. In him humanity's ultimate destiny is already achieved: union with God, sharing his life, full and intimate *communion*.

Jesus puts the present into perspective by casting upon it the light of the future. From the event of Christ onwards, everything else has to be scrutinized, and each generation, each culture, each person has to critically examine its present in the light of that future. Thus the incoming of God in history does not destroy humanity's liberty of decision, each person's responsibility for building the world, but rather liberates his or her liberty, and therefore his or her responsibility, to build a world in accordance with the master plan of God revealed in Jesus Christ. There can therefore be no dichotomy between a human being's love for God and love for the world, between service of God and service of the world. To serve the world is to participate in its growth process, to help in some way to fulfill it, to bring about its true goal—and in doing this we are serving God. To proclaim the Good News of Jesus Christ is precisely to proclaim to the world the secret for its own growth and development as a human world that has a divine origin and a divine destiny. The event of Jesus Christ is what gives true direction and sense to all humanity's striving for a better world. It gives humanity the courage to continue the struggle despite the apparent on-going victory of death. Christ is the "first fruits of those who have died" (1 Cor 15:20). Jesus' proclamation of the Kingdom is the ground of our hope.[25]

Because we believe in the coming Kingdom of God, we cannot cross our arms before the ills of this world, but must become involved in the struggle for a more just and peaceful world. As Paul Tillich pointed out, a true understanding of the Kingdom of God must take into account its political and social connotations.[26]

[25]In this connection, Jurgen Moltmann's classic work, *Theology of Hope: On the Ground and Implications of a Christian Eschatology* (New York: Harper, 1967) is essential reading.

[26]See his *Systematic Theology* (Chicago: University of Chicago, 1963) especially vol. III, 297–423.

This future orientation of the Kingdom, the *eschatological* aspect reminds us that the Kingdom is never to be identified with this world, or any historical manifestation of it. At the same time the hidden grace of the in-coming Kingdom is already at work, and enables men and women to work for a human future that is also God's future. That is why fighting for a better world, where there is greater justice, greater brotherhood and sisterhood, greater tolerance, greater freedom for each human being to grow as a person, to develop his or her potentialities, is an integral part of "seeking" the Kingdom of God. It is not a pure spiritual reality, but involves every aspect of human existence, political, economic, social, educational, etc. Anything that enslaves the human person must be denounced courageously and without fear, and anything that enables the human person to grow must be actively promoted. Only if we do this can we call ourselves "Kingdom people."

Over and over again Jesus underlined by word and action that the coming of the Kingdom was a challenge to our commitment to building a better world, whether it was in the fight against sickness (Luke 13:10-17) or hunger (Luke 6:1-2), unjust traditions (Matt 15:1-14) and regulations (Matt 23:4), political domination (Mark 10:42), the iniquities of the law (Luke 18:2-5), or plain cheating (Luke 16:19-31). To be a Kingdom person is to be a person committed to building a better world, to join in the struggle for true liberation, liberation from sin and all manifestations of it either in ourselves or in society. To be a Kingdom person is to live in the knowledge that God is present in our world, active in it, and that therefore God has not finished with it.

Consequently, despite all the negativities we encounter, there is always hope. The God who sent the Son into history to bring it to salvation is the unshakable ground of that hope—a hope that goes beyond all sin, evil, suffering, and even death. If God took our world so seriously, who are we to take it with less seriousness. The power of the Kingdom—even though invisible to us, hidden from us—is active within the world and within history and it is none other than the power of the Almighty. Its presence is like a Voice calling us from the center of reality to be what God wants us to be, what God has created us to be, and to bring our world to its fullness in God.

We repeat therefore that it demands, in the first place, conversion. We must let the light of the Kingdom, shining from Christ, enter into our hearts and change them. The Kingdom must be our first and guiding preoccupation: "But strive first for the kingdom of God and his righteousness, and all these things will be given to you as well" (Matt 6:33).

Only in this way will we be fit for the Kingdom, and collaborators in its coming. "Thy Kingdom come . . . ." is not just a petition in the Our Father, it is also a program of action, a program of life, it is our mission. For the missionary life of a Christian is the living out in one's life of that petition, collaborating with God in the coming of the Kingdom to its fulfillment, bringing God's plan of salvation to its glorious completion. To do that we must become "new," we must let the Spirit of God make us new, make us free, for we must clothe ourselves "with the new self, created according to the likeness of God in true righteousness and holiness" (Eph 4:24).

This brings home the point that the Kingdom is precisely the Kingdom of *God,* and from *God.* It is not just this world come to its natural fulfillment—it will surpass it infinitely. We realize that the Kingdom is a *gift* from God, a gift that must be welcomed and received with gratitude. It is a deliverance that surpasses anything that a human being can imagine:

> What no eye has seen, nor ear heard
>   nor the human heart conceived,
> what God has prepared for those who love him (1 Cor 2:9).

Jesus emphasized this difference between the Kingdom of God here below and its final realization in the end-time in the parable of the seed:

> He also said, "The kingdom of God is as if someone would scatter seed on the ground, and would sleep and rise night and day, and the seed would sprout and grow, he does not know how. The earth produces of itself, first the stalk, then the head, then the full grain in the head" (Mark 4:26-28).

What is emphasized is the mysterious growth, and the disparity between what is sown and what is reaped. We find the same lesson in the next parable:

> He also said, "With what can we compare the kingdom of God, or what parable will we use for it? It is like a mustard seed, which, when sown upon the ground, is the smallest of all the seeds on earth; yet when it is sown it grows up and becomes the greatest of all shrubs, and puts forth large branches, so that the birds of the air can make nests in its shade" (Mark 4:30-32).

What the missionary must do is sow the seed of the Kingdom in the hearts of the men and women of the world— and in practice this means sowing Jesus Christ in their hearts. We can truthfully see Jesus as being both the seed of the Kingdom and its first fruit. Our goal is that soon his Kingdom will come to the whole world, and he will be "All in all": "When all things are subjected to him, then the Son himself will also be subjected to the one who put all things in subjection under him, so that God may be all in all" (1 Cor 15:28).

Seeing Jesus from the point of view of the Kingdom enables us to see him from a perspective of the future. When we looked at Jesus as the one "sent by the Father," we contemplated him from the perspective of the beginning. When we look at him as the embodiment of the Kingdom, we see him as it were from the perspective of the end, of the *eschaton*. And it is this image, this goal that is the powerful force sustaining humanity in hope, in its constant striving to grow, to be. The Kingdom brought by Christ is the magnet drawing humanity upward to its fullness. Both perspectives are necessary and complement each other.[27] To conclude this section let us make our own the prayer of the author of the Letter to the Ephesians:

> For this reason I bow my knees before the Father, from whom every family in heaven and on earth takes its name. I pray that, according to the riches of his glory, he may grant that you may

---

[27]See Jurgen Moltmann, *The Future of Creation. Collected Essays* (Philadelphia: Fortress, 1979) especially 86–8.

be strengthened in your inner being with power through his Spirit, and that Christ may dwell in your hearts through faith, as you are being rooted and grounded in love. I pray that you may have the power to comprehend, with all the saints, what is the breadth and length and height and depth, and to know the love of Christ that surpasses knowledge, so that you may be filled with all the fullness of God (3:14-19).

CHAPTER 5

Christ, the Savior

In looking at the Kingdom of God as proclaimed by Jesus Christ, we saw that, from the point of view of humanity and our entry into the Kingdom, Jesus uses the phrase almost as a synonym for what we understand as salvation: it sums up the divine salvation that will reach its climax with the coming of Christ in glory at the end of history. To say that "The Kingdom of God is close at hand" is, therefore, in so far as its proximity has a bearing on our lives, another way of saying that salvation is near to us. Entry into the Kingdom means that one enters into the process of salvation, that one is being saved, that one has "entered into eternal life." The intimate connection between salvation and the Kingdom of God is underlined for example in Mark 10:24-27:

> But Jesus said to them again, "Children, how hard it is to enter the kingdom of God! It is easier for a camel to go through the eye of a needle than for someone who is rich to enter the kingdom of God." They were greatly astounded and said to one another, "Then who can be saved?" Jesus looked at them and said, "For mortals it is impossible, but not for God; for God all things are possible."[1]

[1]See: *Theological Dictionary of the New Testament,* Gerhard Friedrich, ed. (Grand Rapids: Eerdmans, 1971) vol. VII, 965–1024. See also the fine article, "Salvation" in *The Concise Sacramentum Mundi* (New York: Crossroad, 1975) 1499–1530.

The words of Jesus, "Blessed are the poor in spirit for theirs is the Kingdom of Heaven" (Matt 5:3) could be paraphrased, "Blessed are the poor in spirit, for salvation belongs to them." The Kingdom of God is God pitching his tent within humanity, giving meaning and therefore hope to humanity's existence. Because of it the imprisoned are now set free, the blind can now see, sinners are forgiven, and death has been conquered. To work for the bringing about of the Kingdom is to be at the service of the salvation process here below, to share in it, both for ourselves and for the world about us. To refuse to enter into the Kingdom is to reject the salvation that is offered to us by God. The Kingdom stands as a powerful image for the reality of salvation, and when salvation is fully accomplished, then God's will is done, and the kingdom of Satan has come to an end.

The world was called into existence in virtue of the universal salvific will of God, because God in God's infinite goodness wished to share with created beings God's own infinite love and happiness. God wants all people "to be saved and come to the knowledge of the truth" (1 Tim 2:4). This immediately underlines that the offer of salvation is present right from the very beginning, and is not just the result of humanity's rejection of God's invitation. To think in this way is to say that humanity would not be saved if humanity had not sinned! What would have been the flow of events if humanity from the beginning had said yes to God's invitation we do not know; all we know is the actual history of salvation that has taken place, and that it is a history of salvation which takes into account humanity's sin. Any other possible history of salvation is purely hypothetical.

Nevertheless, even in this hypothetical case, we do know that salvation would still have been a reality, for God does not repent of having created. God was not obligated to create us, did not have to share the eternal, infinitely perfect divine happiness with creatures. The fact that God does is precisely the unmerited blessing which he bestows on creation, and this is the first and ever permanent aspect of salvation: the bestowal of a blessing the dimensions of which surpass even our wildest dreams, a blessing that is totally and completely unmerited and that springs from the absolute goodness and absolute generosity of the God who created us in love. Salvation is the pouring out on us of God's infinite love, sharing that love with personal beings whom he himself has called into existence. John brings this out wonderfully in his First Letter: "And we have seen and do testify that the Father has sent his Son as the Savior of the world" (4:14).

Salvation is total gift. So that while we can say that salvation first conjures up the idea of rescue from an imminent threat to our lives, the deeper meaning of salvation infinitely surpasses that: the rescue aspect is but the first step in the bestowal of a blessing that surpasses anything that we could possibly imagine, for

> no eye has seen, nor ear heard,
> nor the human heart conceived,
> what God has prepared for those
> who love him (1 Cor 2:9; Isa 64:4).

Salvation is entry into nothing less than the infinite happiness, infinite life of God. It is to be caught up in the infinite eternal communion of love that is the intimate being of the Godself.

This calls to mind the eschatological aspect of salvation—it is something that still awaits fulfillment. It will be completed in the "last age." This last age is *already* inaugurated in Christ, but has yet to be completed. Like the Kingdom it is *already* at work in the world, but still its ultimate and glorious manifestation remains hidden. We must still groan and labor under the weight of sin, under the fallen condition in which we find ourselves, "for here we have no lasting city, but we are looking for the city that is to come" (Heb 13:14). However, because of Jesus Christ not even the enormity of sin and its consequences which we see within us and around us can destroy our hope, "for just as by the one man's disobedience the many were made sinners, so by the one man's obedience the many will be made righteous" (Rom 5:18-20). Humanity can look forward to salvation and constantly strive to attain it knowing in faith that it does not strive after the non-existent or the impossible.

Even in this present life salvation is experienced—at least to a degree. It is experienced every time we are empowered to move out of our egoism, out of our own sinfulness, and to live love—that is, to live for God, for one another, and for creation. It is experienced when one is enabled to break down the walls of self-centeredness and selfishness that surround the human heart and open oneself in self-giving to others. It is experienced when one is able to enter into the message of the Good News and accept it with joy and gratitude. There is a present reality but one that is stretching forward in a deep longing for fulfillment. This tension between present and future is common in all New Testament theology.

Furthermore, salvation is not something that affects the soul alone, or the body alone, but rather affects the whole person, mind and heart, body and soul. This does not come out clearly in the English word "save" but is very clear in the original New Testament word of *sozein*. It is true that very often we find the word used in connection with the preservation, the maintenance, and the healing of physical life (e.g., Mark 5:23, 28; Matt 8:25; 14:30). But there are other occasions in which Jesus uses the word to signify something beyond that, as for example when he says to the sinner who had wiped his feet with her hair: "Your faith has saved you; go in peace" (Luke 7:50). Here he obviously refers to something more than the restoration of bodily health, for here there was no preceding bodily sickness and therefore no bodily cure. When Jesus brings salvation, it is always to the whole person.

And not only does salvation affect the person in his or her individual existence; it also has repercussions on society. Just as evil had and has dire repercussions on humankind, on individuals in the deepest aspects of their personal lives, affecting our relationship with God, with the neighbor and with infra-human creation, so likewise salvation affects the whole human being, in one's personal and social identity. To say that salvation is something purely individual, personal, is to deny the social nature of the human person and also to deny the social repercussions of sin and evil. Contrariwise, to say that salvation is purely social, something that affects humanity only as a totality, is to deny the personal foundation of sin and evil. Both aspects must be kept in mind.

Salvation understood as a blessing, the original blessing of God on the world, manifests itself first of all in creation. In the opening chapter of the Bible, we hear the refrain: "And God saw that it was good." The goodness of creation is constantly affirmed, the original blessing repeatedly referred to, and the chapter closes with the words: "God saw everything that he had made, and indeed, it was very good" (Gen 1:31). It is easy to forget that each and every human being is created in the image and likeness of God, an image and likeness that even sin has not completely destroyed. It would be totally unrealistic to deny the presence of sin in human life, but to declare that sin has totally defaced the image of God in humans is ultimately to declare than human beings are totally incapable of recognizing the presence of God in the created order and therefore incapable of recognizing God in Jesus Christ. It is important to recall this truth for so often we forget it, and when we do so we should not be surprised that we then are inclined to see salvation, as I have said, exclusively in terms of rescue, in terms of being *saved from* a disaster, rather than being *saved into* an infinitely graced existence.

Even though Israel quite early on began to see salvation exclusively in terms of its own history, in terms of God's working with them alone, yet there are clear indications in Scripture that salvation had much wider horizons. Many theologians will refer, for example, to the covenant made with Noah and through him with all creation:

> Then God said to Noah and to his sons with him, "As for me, I am establishing my covenant with you and your descendants after you, and with every living creature that is with you, the birds, the domestic animals, and every animal of the earth with you, as many as came out of the ark. I establish my covenant with you, that never again shall all flesh be cut off by the waters of a flood, and never again shall there be a flood to destroy the earth." God said, "This is the sign of the covenant that I make

between me and you and every living creature that is with you,
for all future generations: I have set my bow in the clouds, and
it shall be a sign of the covenant between me and the earth"
(Gen 9:8-13).

Apart from this there are other clear indications that salvation extended beyond the narrow boundaries of Israel. For
example we have the Book of Jonah, which is a beautiful
testimony of Yahweh's all embracing love and which concludes
with the words:

And should I not be concerned about Nineveh, that great city,
in which there are more than a hundred and twenty thousand
persons who do not know their right hand from their left, and
also many animals? (4:11).

God's mercy is not to be confined or limited by human
interpretations, human preconceptions of what salvation is all
about. We are reminded of the Lord's parable about the
workers in the vineyard who would like to confine the goodness of the owner to their own ideas of justice: "Am I not
allowed to do what I choose with what belongs to me? Or are
you envious because I am generous?" (Matt 20:15).

The Wisdom literature of the Bible is particularly rich in
underlining the universal scope of salvation—something
which Wisdom tends to describe by the term "life."

For whoever finds me finds life
    and obtains favor from the Lord;
but those who miss me injure themselves;
    all who hate me love death (Prov 8:35-36).

Salvation is not an "it" but it is a "Thou" a "life." It is
nothing other than the Godself breaking into creation, taking
creation into the Godself. Salvation is God with us, is
Emmanuel, is Jesus. "And remember, I am with you always,
to the end of the age" (Matt 28:20b).

Wisdom in the Bible is portrayed as existing before creation,
participating in the creative process, open towards creation
and seeking the realization of all its potentiality. Without

entering into the discussion of the precise nature of the personification of Wisdom in the biblical tradition, we can say that it represents God in God's preoccupation for the happiness of humanity. In the Book of Wisdom we are reminded that God loves all that has been created:

> For you love all things that exist,
> and detest none of the things you have made,
> for you would not have made anything if you had hated it.
> How would anything have endured if you had not willed it?
> Or how would anything not called forth by you have been
>   preserved?
> You spare all things for they are yours, O Lord,
> you who love the living.
> For your immortal spirit is in all things (11:24–12:1).

And because of this, God's mercy extends to all nations:

> For neither is there any God besides you,
> whose care is for all people,
> to whom you should prove that you have not judged unjustly;
> Nor can any king or monarch confront you about those
> whom you have punished.
> You are righteous and you rule all things righteously,
> deeming it alien to your power
> to condemn anyone who does not deserve to be punished
> (Wis 12:13-15).

To have life is the beginning of salvation; to be called into life is to be called into God's plan of salvation; to have one's life rescued when it is threatened is to experience salvation in a concrete way; to enter into the fullness of life, where it is no longer subject to death or decay, no longer subject to threat of any kind—that is definitive salvation, fullness of salvation, that is "everlasting life." And that is the salvation that Christ came to bring us: "I came that they may have life, and have it abundantly" (John 10:10). In him, the salvation of God is manifested—demons are driven out: "If it is by the finger of God that I cast out the demons, then the kingdom of God has come to you" (Luke 11:20; cf. 10:17-18), sinners are reconciled with God, the poor are especially blessed, those who have strayed are gathered in. For that reason the Good News of Jesus Christ is called "the message of this salvation" (Acts 13:26), "a way of salvation" (Acts 16:17), "the power of God for salvation" (Rom 1:16).

And yet the fact that we forget our "original blessing" is understandable. We live in a very obviously fallen world. A few minutes reflection is sufficient to show us that there is something very, very wrong with our world. More than ever before in the history of the universe we realize the terrible and frightening division within humanity itself, between humanity and its environment, and between humanity and God. Vatican II in its constitution on The Church in the Modern World put it like this:

> What revelation makes known to us is confirmed by our own experience. For when man looks into his own heart he finds that he is drawn towards what is wrong and sunk in many evils which cannot come from his good creator. Often refusing to acknowledge God as his source, man has also upset the relationship which should link him to his last end; and at the same time he has broken the right order that should reign within himself as well as between himself and other men and all creatures. Man therefore is divided in himself. As a result the whole life of men, both individual and social, shows itself to be a struggle, and a dramatic one, between good and evil, between light and darkness (no. 13).

The message of salvation enters into our situation of alienation, our situation of radical frustration, bringing acceptance, hope, joy, and peace. Usually we reserve the word "damnation" for the ultimate consequence of rejecting God, something that will possibly take place after this life, but damnation is to a certain extent experienced here and now, in the alienation we experience within our own being, in sickness, age, and the process of dying, the alienation we experience in our relationship with others, in the broken friendships, the misunderstandings, the antipathies and disappointments of everyday life, and in the alienation we experience in our relationship with God, in our guilt and sense of sin. For damnation is the definitive experience of alienation, while salvation is the definitive experience of acceptance, of wholeness, of peace in the deepest sense. In this world we experience both, but our faith gives us the assurance that damnation is not and will not be the winner, because through Christ the decisive battle of salvation has been fought and won.

Perhaps in the past we have so emphasized man's fallen nature that we have been inclined to see it as being utterly hopeless, so that we were inclined to think that prior to the coming of Christ there was no goodness in the world, no grace. At the same time we must not espouse the opposite danger, that of so emphasizing the ever permanent presence of grace and the Spirit of God that we fail to appreciate the absolute centrality of the life, death, and resurrection of Christ in the history of salvation. Jesus Christ is the absolute Mediator, and in his paschal mystery the new and eternal covenant between God and humanity has been signed and sealed.

However, the radical definitiveness of the new covenant does not deny its continuity with the covenants that preceded it. The new covenant fulfills what was promised in the old covenant. The original promise of blessing at the beginning of creation achieves its manifestation and realization in the paschal mystery of Jesus Christ. The two aspects must always be kept in mind, and this is particularly important for the missionary. If the original blessing is so emphasized that the centrality of Christ is not seen, then very soon the missionary zeal will diminish and disappear. If the centrality of Christ is so emphasized that the original blessing is totally destroyed, then true and deep inculturation of the Good News in each given culture will become extremely difficult. An understanding of Christ the Savior will help us in this context, help to maintain our zeal and our hope.

The theme of salvation is found in all the New Testament writings, and it is significant that the verb "to save" is used no less than 106 times, while the noun "salvation" is found 45 times. For example, in the Gospel of Matthew, Jesus is portrayed right from the very beginning in terms of salvation: "She will bear a son, and you are to name him Jesus, for he will save his people from their sins" (1:21).

The name "Jesus" means literally "God is salvation." Cullmann tells us that "this proper name is one of the Hebrew forms of the title 'Savior' applied to God in the Old Testament."[2] And he goes on to explain that in the Old Testament salvation emphasized deliverance from sin and death. The authors of the New Testament would have been very conscious of this and for that reason "just as the original source of the *Kyrios* title for Jesus lies primarily in Judaism, so it is more likely that his designation of *Soter* (Savior) is connected with the Jewish and Old Testament concept rather than the Hellenistic one."[3]

Every page of the Bible speaks to us in some way about salvation. The *Benedictus* of Zechariah is a sort of commentary on all the events surrounding the Incarnation, which heralded the coming of the fulfillment of the promises, the inauguration of the final era of the history of salvation. And it is the supreme New Testament prayer of thanksgiving for the gift of salvation.

The angels proclaim to the shepherds: "To you is born this day in the city of David a Savior, who is the Messiah the Lord" (Luke 2:11). Despite the fact that the term was used for the Roman emperor and other rulers, Luke does not hesitate to apply it to Jesus in the widest sense possible. The old man Simeon with the Christ child in his arms, gives thanks to God "for my eyes have seen your salvation" (Luke 2:30). Jesus is not just the bringer of salvation, the announcer of salvation, the messenger of salvation. He is himself the salvation; in him salvation becomes incarnate—and this salvation is prepared by God "in the presence of all peoples, a light for revelation to the Gentiles, and for glory to your people Israel" (Luke 2:31-32). John the Baptizer prepared for the entrance of Jesus in the public arena by inviting the people to repen-

---

[2]O. Cullmann, *The Christology of the New Testament* (Philadelphia: Westminster, 1963) 242.
[3]Ibid. 241.

tance, for the time is come and "all flesh shall see the salvation of God," not just the inspired Simeon. In the Gospel this centrality of Jesus as the bringer of salvation is probably best expressed by his words to Zacchaeus, the tax collector: "Today salvation has come to this house, because he too is a son of Abraham. For the Son of man came to seek out and to save the lost" (Luke 19:9-10).

If Luke had any reticence in naming Jesus as the Savior in his first volume, there was no such reticence in his second volume. In Acts Jesus is clearly the Savior of the world:

> There is salvation in no one else, for there is no other name under heaven given among mortals by which we must be saved (4:12).

> God exalted him at his right hand as Leader and Savior (5:31).

In John's Gospel, Jesus is called "The Savior of the world" (4:42), and the fact that the title was one used by the Roman emperor would seem to suggest that the imperial association was intended.[4] The detail that this proclamation is made by the Samaritans underlines the universal application of the title, as well as the kingly nuances implied. Jesus is the absolute bringer of salvation.

Paul declared openly to the synagogue of Antioch of Pisidia: "Of this man's [David] posterity God has brought to Israel a Savior, Jesus, as he promised" (Acts 13:23). Paul's whole aim was to bring the saving work of Christ to others. He instructs his young churches not to give "offense to Jews or to Greeks or to the church of God, just as I try to please everyone in everything I do, not seeking my own advantage, but that of many, so that they may be saved" (1 Cor 10:32-33). And not just to the Gentiles, but also to his fellow Jews: "Brothers and sisters, my heart's desire and prayer to God for them is that they may be saved" (Rom 10:1).

---

[4]See Craig R. Koester, "The Savior of the World" (John 4:42) in *Journal of Biblical Literature* (vol. 109/4. 1990) 665–80.

Paul was convinced that salvation was taking place in the world according to a plan, a plan that stretches from the first moment of creation to the final moment when God will be "all in all" (a point that is fully brought out by the author of the Letter to the Ephesians, cf. 3:1-19). And not only does it stretch from creation to the consummation of the world, but likewise embraces all, for the Good News of Jesus Christ, "is the power of God for salvation to everyone who has faith, to the Jew first and also to the Greek" (Rom 1:16), "for there is no distinction between Jew and Greek; the same Lord is Lord of all and is generous to all who call on him" (Rom 10:12). The gift of salvation lies at the heart of creation, for this we were destined by God from the very beginning: "For God has destined us not for wrath, but for obtaining salvation through our Lord Jesus Christ" (1 Thess 5:9).

God is the great architect of salvation and to work it out in practice he has, as it were, his blueprint. The heart, the center, the high point of this plan is Jesus Christ. In the opening chapter of his First Letter to the Corinthians, Paul writes:

> For since, in the wisdom of God, the world did not know God through wisdom, God decided, through the foolishness of our proclamation, to save those who believe. For Jews demand signs and Greeks desire wisdom, but we proclaim Christ crucified, a stumbling block to Jews and foolishness to Gentiles, but to those who are the called, both Jews and Greeks, Christ the power of God and the wisdom of God. For God's foolishness is wiser than human wisdom, and God's weakness is stronger than human strength (1:21-25).

According to Joseph A. Fitzmyer[5] here is to be sought "the key to Pauline theology." Salvation in Jesus Christ is at the heart of the Gospel as preached by Paul. For Paul Jesus Christ is the Lord of creation in the fullest sense, as is proclaimed in

---

[5]See *The New Jerome Biblical Commentary* (Englewood Cliffs, N.J.: Prentice Hall, 1990) 1388.

the great christological passage of Colossians 1:15-20: "He is the image of the invisible God, the first-born of all creation; for in him all things were created, in heaven and on earth, visible and invisible. . . ." (v. 15).

Paul's understanding of salvation is for the most part conveyed by a series of metaphors, which tend to describe what he means by salvation rather than give an analytical analysis of it. He chooses metaphors borrowed from human activities. This must be constantly remembered, for if we carry the metaphors too far, then we can easily end up with unacceptable distortions. He talks about "reconciliation," *(katallage)*. Without Christ the world stands alienated from God, no longer at peace, and Christ comes with his peace, "reconciling the world" with God:

> In Christ God was reconciling the world to himself, not counting their trespasses against them, and entrusting the message of reconciliation to us (2 Cor 5:19; cf. Rom 5:10).

It is important to note that in reconciliation God always maintains the initiative, it is he who reconciles us to himself. Through Christ a profound change is effected in us, a change by means of which we become new, and in this change we are reconciled to God. There is no change in God. At the same time this change is not imposed on us but God enables us to enter actively into the reconciliation process. His grace builds on our nature and raises it so that we can personally enter into the reconciliation.

Reconciliation brings it about that humanity is purified of its sin by Christ, who, as it were, offers the expiatory sacrifice of himself on our behalf. The metaphor of *expiation* has nothing to do with the placating of an angry God, or offering "propitiation" to God—as if God were an object. Rather it refers to the purification of sinful humanity:

> Since all have sinned and fall short of the glory of God, they are justified by his grace as a gift, through the redemption that is in Christ Jesus, whom God put forward as a sacrifice of atonement by his blood, effective through faith (Rom 3:23-25).

It is not God who is made gracious in forgiveness by the "expiation" of Christ, but rather by it sinful humanity is changed radically.

In this way *we are redeemed*,[6] liberated from our captivity, our slavery. Entering into Christ, into his service, is entry into freedom. Through Christ we are justified. Here Paul calls on the court of law for his metaphor. The sentence that has been passed on one who believes in Christ is one of acquittal. He reminds the Corinthians that the "word of the cross is folly to those who are perishing, but to us who are being saved it is the power of God" (1 Cor 1:18) and that they are "the aroma of Christ to God among those who are being saved and among those who are perishing, to one a fragrance from death to death, to the other a fragrance from life to life" (2 Cor 2:15-16). It must be emphasized that redemption in Paul is not something that exists apart from Christ but is achieved by entry into him. The measure of our entry into Christ, the measure of our "putting on Christ" is the measure of our redemption. When we have totally put on Christ, then is our redemption complete and definitive.

> He has rescued us from the power of darkness and transferred us to the kingdom of his beloved Son, in whom we have redemption, the forgiveness of sins (Col 1:13-14).

---

[6]The metaphor of "redemption" *(apolutrosis)* is very close to that of "ransom" *(lutron)*, which we find in Mark's Gospel, "the Son of Man came not to be served but to serve, and to give his life a ransom for many" (10:45). This metaphor was developed in patristic writings, and unfortunately, in a rather detailed and crude way. They began by asking such questions as "To whom is the ransom to be paid?" "Could it be paid to God?" or "Was the Devil the recipient of the ransom?" The ransom idea was further developed in the feudal period—an age when the Devil began to acquire strict rights, and the whole drama of salvation was presented as a powerful feudal epic. Anselm, after demolishing the theory of redemption based on the Devil's "rights," replaced it with a doctrine of strict juridical satisfaction based on the two natures of Christ. He bases his theory of salvation on the idea that sin had deeply injured God's majesty and honor—a damage that could only be undone by God himself, and that ought to be undone by humanity—a dilemma that was

> In him we have redemption through his blood, the forgiveness of our trespasses, according to the riches of his grace that he lavished upon us (Eph 1:7-8).

Salvation is the culmination of the reconciliation process: "For if while we were enemies we were reconciled to God through the death of his Son, much more surely, having been reconciled, will we be saved by his life" (Rom 5:10).

And glorification is the culmination of the salvation process: "And those whom he justified he also glorified" (Rom 8:30).

In our present situation, "All have sinned and fall short of the glory of God" (Rom 3:23). For the Christian salvation consists in obtaining "the glory of our Lord Jesus Christ" (2 Thess 2:14) for

> our citizenship is in heaven, and it is from there that we are expecting a Savior, the Lord Jesus Christ. He will transform the body of our humiliation that it may be conformed to the body of his glory, by the power that also enables him to make all things subject to himself (Phil 3:20-21).

We can see therefore that in Paul salvation is much more than salvation *from* something: it is primarily salvation *to* something, for he holds that salvation is rather the filling of a void than the escape from a chasm. As Christians we are awaiting God's "Son from heaven, whom he raised from the dead, Jesus who delivers us from the wrath to come" (1 Thess 1:10). In this there is for Paul a close correspondence between the eschatological Son of Man and Savior.[7]

Paul sees salvation as the actualization of the potentiality for wholeness, for completeness enclosed in the Gospel, the

---

solved by the Incarnation. His theory was very legalistic, and God's love manifest in the salvation of humanity receded into the background. It was also open to the charge of being extrinsic, and somewhat mechanical. The metaphor of "ransom" when carried too deeply into the legal or banking areas suggest the idea of calculation, of quantification—something that is totally foreign to the Gospel.

[7] See Bultmann, *Theology of the New Testament*, I, 79–80.

Good News. Salvation comes about because Christ inserts himself within the very heart of humanity, the innermost core of human existence, and in his life, death, and resurrection Christ becomes the "future Adam," of whom the first Adam was but a type (Rom 5:14). Through Christ humanity is once again made capable of recovering the image in which it is created; once more, each individual human being is made capable of "becoming like God." Jesus assumes all that it means to be human, all the desires for fullness, for wholeness, all the experience of being under the load of sin, imprisoned inside the limitations imposed by each person's sin both as an individual and as a social being, and in responding perfectly to God releases humanity from this imprisonment, thus empowering it to once more achieve its deepest desires, once more attain its full realization.

In bringing himself to fulfillment, symbolized in the resurrection, fulfillment for all humanity is possible, and that fulfillment is nothing less than union with God. Salvation will achieve its complete realization in the eschaton, when "we all attain to the unity of the faith and of the knowledge of the Son of God, to mature manhood, to the measure of the stature of the fullness of Christ" (Eph 4:13). Jesus Christ is, as it were, the model used for the creation of humankind. If the human person is created in the image and likeness of God, Jesus Christ is the very model. He is the *Imago Dei* in humanity (and this does not imply any superiority of male over female—for both share equally in humanity!).

The traditions of the Eastern churches give full expression to this concept of salvation, and in it we find such words as *theosis* (becoming God or "deification") and *theopoiesis* (being made God).[8] For them, salvation is nothing less than "deification," precisely because it is definitive entry into the *very life of God*. To be united with Christ is to become like him. What they mean by this is that humanity, because of Christ, can once

---

[8]See, for example, Donald F. Winslow, *The Dynamic of Salvation: A Study in Gregory of Nazianzus* (Philadelphia: Philadelphia Patristic Foundation, 1979).

again become like God, not by nature, but by grace. By our own efforts human beings are totally incapable of entering into the life of the Father, the life of God, but God the Father stretches out as it were, in Christ, in order to invite us and capacitate us to enter into and share that divine life, that divine love. We do not of course share God's *essence,* (such an idea would be blasphemous!) but we do enter into his immortal life and happiness.[9] According to nature we remain human, but according to grace, we enter into the divine life of our heavenly Father. There is here reality but not identity. Reference is often made to the Second Letter of Peter:

> His divine power has given us everything needed for life and godliness, through the knowledge of him who called us by his own glory and goodness. Thus he has given us, through these things, his precious and very great promises, so that through them you may escape from the corruption that is in the world because of lust, and may become participants of the divine nature (1:3-4).

Within the Western tradition of the Church, this idea also finds an echo. For example, in the Mass we pray: "By the mystery of this water and wine may we come to share in the divinity of Christ, who humbled himself to share in our humanity." The entry of the Second Person of the Blessed Trinity into the world, the taking to himself of human nature, underlines the potentiality of human nature for "deification."

Furthermore, this process of "deification" is not something that will take place only with our resurrection, but is already taking place in the measure in which we conform our minds to the mind of God the Father, thus becoming ever more "Godlike."

[9]The magnificent work of the late Karl Rahner on the nature of grace and its relation with nature has helped us to better appreciate the notion of "deification." Because human nature has a "supernatural existential," we have, through our graced creation, the potentiality to share the divine life, and through the same grace-redeeming activity of Christ, all obstacles to that sharing are removed.

We generally tend to avoid the word *theosis* because of its possible pantheistic misinterpretation, or because it sounds so arrogant, but in doing so do we not miss something vital in our understanding of salvation? Do we tend to forget that we are from the very beginning destined for *communion* with God who is our Father, the God who in Jesus Christ has adopted us as sons and daughters? Do we forget that the whole Christian journey is precisely oriented towards that goal, towards communion in God's own life? In emphasizing humanity's distinction from God—God is indeed the totally Other—do we perhaps forget thereby the extraordinary aspect of God's gift of grace and its relation to us? There is a tendency for us to express salvation in terms of bringing humanity to its fullness, but in doing so we can forget that that fullness is precisely a fullness that is supernatural, a fullness that is pure grace, pure gift, totally and completely unmerited by us, for it is nothing less than entry into communion with the divine life, a fullness that is attained, and can only be attained, in and through the grace of Christ. The concept of salvation as deification, rightly and carefully understood, brings out in a wondrous way the absolute gratuity of salvation, the awesomeness of our ultimate vocation, and the consequent need for eucharist and liturgy, for thanksgiving and adoration.

The profound insight that salvation is "deification" by grace, is particularly helpful, I feel, when preaching salvation in the African context, for there the intimate connection between humanity and God is deeply embedded in the African soul. To prescind from the vertical dimension of salvation is ultimately to be untrue to it. By the term *theosis,* therefore, we are reminded that salvation is something that infinitely surpasses our expectations, a gift that comes exclusively from God.

At the same time it must not be forgotten that salvation also has a horizontal dimension. This has been stressed very much in our own time, especially by the Liberation theologians of Latin America. For many, liberation and salvation are synonymous terms. Salvation comes to us when we are liberated from the bonds of sin, the bonds of egoism, and empowered to be what we are called to be, the fully free sons and daughters of God, reflecting in our lives his image. This liberation is something that must affect our whole being, affect us in our individuality and in our social/political constitution. Salvation as liberation emphasizes that this world is the theater in which the drama of salvation is to be worked out. It demands commitment to building a better world, a world more in conformity with the God in whose image we are created. True Christianity must be lived everywhere, in our homes, in our places of work and recreation, and not just in the Church. It must be lived each and every day and not just for an hour on Sunday mornings.

At the same time Christianity must be nourished by the formal exercise of prayer and reflection, and it must be celebrated in the community. The latter may seem purely "spiritual" exercises, but it is they that sustain the other "mundane" exercises; similarly the "mundane" must be brought under the influence of the Spirit if they are to be truly Christian. For the Christian the dichotomy between the mundane and the spiritual is false. When they are separated we find a distortion of the Christian life that is extremely dangerous—resulting in gross materialism on the one hand, and pietistic escapism on the other. Salvation comes to the whole person in his or her physical, spiritual, affective, moral, social, and political orientations.

To put the same thing in another way, we can say that, the horizontal and the vertical aspects of salvation must not be separated. To overemphasize the vertical aspect can lead to an unacceptable spiritualism, to a subtle "opium" that can lead to indifferentism regarding this world and our responsibility for it, regarding justice and peace—and for the Christian, conscious of the fundamental command of love that is never permissible. To overemphasize the horizontal can lead to an over preoccupation with this world, with the secular, to the exclusion of God—something that usually leads to a "deification" of this world or some aspect of it, to idolatry.

The two aspects find their expression in the cross of Jesus. The vertical and horizontal poles of the cross are a beautiful sign of the wholeness of salvation as revealed in Jesus Christ.

Take away one of the planks, and we no longer have a cross, and without the Cross we no longer have *Christian* salvation.

The dynamism of salvation enters into all cultures enabling them to realize all that is best within them, freeing them from all that would diminish them, all that would make them less than fully human. In Christ, missionaries too are called to be saviors to those to whom they are sent. As bearers of the Good News of Jesus Christ, missionaries are harbingers of hope, that hope which assures people that the ultimate source of their existence is good, is life affirming, and therefore that life itself is meaningful. The missionaries of Jesus Christ can proclaim this Good News with security for in their faith they know that this hope has already been realized in the resurrection of our Savior. Paul had no hesitation in uniting the two ideas of "apostle" and "saving": for example in Romans he writes: "Now I am speaking to you Gentiles. Inasmuch then as I am an apostle to the Gentiles, I glorify my ministry in order to make my own people jealous, and thus save some of them" (11:13-14). And again, "For though I am free from all men, I have made myself a slave to all, that I might win the more" (1 Cor 9:19).

To be a "savior" to others in Jesus Christ, one must first enter into Jesus and then enter into the heart of others, enter into their culture, their hopes, their aspirations, into their need, their pain, their suffering. In other words one must allow Christ to live in us so that he can go and be present in a visible way to them in us. That is why each generation and each culture must discover Christ for itself. Each situation will bring forth the emphasis needed. What is important for the missionary is to be sensitive to the signs of the times and to the wholeness of the message he is sent to proclaim. When one talks about missionary work, the work of salvation, then one necessarily comes into contact with the absolute need of identifying with Christ. The well-known claim of Paul "it is no longer I who live, but it is Christ who lives in me" (Gal 2:20) is not just a statement of a relationship, but a description of a dynamic spirituality. It must be the description of the ultimate goal and daily struggle of every Christian missionary.

We must *be* Good News for others, and we will be so in the measure in which we allow Christ to live in us. In him we can do all things; apart from him we can do nothing. And like him, the missionary must be prepared to love the other as Christ did, even to death on a cross.

CHAPTER 6

Son of Man

We now come to examine another title which throws further light on the saving mission of Jesus: the title "Son of Man." Exegetes have debated over whether the title as such originated with Jesus himself, or whether it originated within the early Christian community. John P. Meier is of the opinion that "the peculiar Son-of-Man locution goes back in some way to Jesus, however much it was developed later by the Church."[1] Whatever the case may be, the writers of the Gospels saw in it a powerful way of expressing their insight into the significance of Jesus Christ for their own lives, and for the proclamation of him to their contemporaries.[2]

It is a rather mysterious title and is found almost exclusively in the Gospels. It occurs in all four of them, and in all the various strands of tradition found therein. Later tradition dropped the title completely, either perhaps because it was not understandable to Gentile audiences or because it could lead too easily to undesirable misinterpretations. It is highly

---

[1] *The New Jerome Biblical Commentary,* Raymond Brown, Joseph Fitzmyer, Roland Murphy, eds. (Englewood Cliffs, N.J.: Prentice Hall, 1990) 1325.

[2] For an overview of modern scholarship on the question, see William O. Walker, Jr. "The Son of Man: Some Recent Developments" in *CBQ* 45 (1983) 584–607; also, John R. Donahue, "Recent Studies on the Origin of 'Son of Man' in the Gospels" in *CBQ* 48 (1986) 484–8.

significant that, in the Gospels, apart from John 12:34, it is not found on any other lips except those of Jesus himself. And this is one of the factors which indicate its origin in the historical Jesus, for as Oscar Cullmann has written:

> If the evangelists were really the first to introduce the title, why do they use it only when they represent Jesus Himself as speaking? They themselves never call him by this name and they never report another's doing so in conversation with Jesus. This would be completely inexplicable if they were really the first to attribute the title to Jesus as a self-designation. Actually, they have preserved the memory that only Jesus himself used it in this way.[3]

There are 86 uses of the term in the New Testament—14 times in Mark, 30 in Matthew, 25 in Luke, and 13 in John, once in Acts, and three times in quotations from the LXX.[4]

Perhaps the evangelists' preference for this title springs precisely from its enigmatic nature, its power to suggest a whole range of ideas. It would seem that even the Palestinian audience had some difficulty in identifying what precisely was meant by the phrase: "The crowd answered him, 'We have heard from the law that the Messiah remains for ever. How can you say that the Son of Man must be lifted up? Who is this Son of Man?'" (John 12:34).

One exegete, I. H. Marshall, who claims that Jesus himself used the title, suggests why he chose it and his ambiguous use of it. He writes that it may have been that Jesus

> avoided overt identification of himself with the Son of Man and so sought to preserve a certain mystery regarding his person. What this mystery was can now be indicated. It has

[3]Oscar Cullmann, *The Christology of the New Testament,* rev. ed. (Philadelphia: Westminster, 1959) 155.

[4]In this number are included all uses, although I am aware that some uses of the title may go back to a misunderstanding of a generic use or where there is another tradition of parallels. See Joachim Jeremias, *New Testament Theology I: The Proclamation of Jesus* (New York: Scribner's, 1971) 266f.

always seemed remarkable that Jesus should have adopted a self-designation for himself which was, so far as we can tell, far from central in Jewish thought and whose use as a title in Aramaic is even a matter of some doubt. The reason for this may be found in the desire of Jesus to give cautious expression to his own unique relationship with God as his Son and agent of salvation. The title Messiah was both inadequate to express this relationship (since the Messiah tends to be an earthly figure of limited authority) and misleading (thanks to popular nationalistic interpretations), while that of Son was only too clear in its implications. But the title of Son of Man had distinct merits. It was admirably fitted to express Jesus' conception of his own person since it referred to a person closely linked with God and of heavenly origin. In this respect it was superior to the title of Messiah. Furthermore, it was not a current term and was capable of being molded by Jesus to suit his own conceptions.[5]

Exegetes[6] have noted a number of different uses of the title:

1. As one who is in solidarity with the whole human race.
2. As the Suffering Son of Man.
3. As the Eschatological Judge of glory.
4. As the One in whom humanity and divinity meet.

We mention these four although in reality the use of the title could be reduced to two:

> Jesus uses the term in two principal ways. On the one hand, he used it to refer to his earthly career as a figure of authority rejected by men, crucified and raised from the dead. On the

---

[5]I. H. Marshall, "The Synoptic Son of Man Sayings in Recent Discussions," in *New Testament Studies* 12 (1965–1966) 350.

[6]See, for example, Heinz Todt, *The Son of Man in the Synoptic Tradition* (Philadelphia, 1965); R. H. Fuller, *The Foundations of New Testament Christology* (Scribner's, 1965) 34–43; R. Bultmann, *Theology of the New Testament,* vol I (London, SCM, 1952) 28–32; O. Cullmann, *The Christology of the New Testament* (Philadelphia: Westminster, 1959) 137–88; Ch. Duquoc, *Christologie* (Paris: Cerf, 1968) 188–209.

other hand, he spoke of a coming Son of man who would act in sovereign power at the last judgement.[7]

However, for the sake of clarity we will examine the title under the four headings mentioned above.

Jesus, One with Us

In the Old Testament the phrase "son of man" was sometimes used as a synonym for the human person, as is clear from the following four quotations, where the phrase as used in synonymous poetic parallelism, forms the second half of the parallel to "man" or "human" in the first half:

> What is man that thou are mindful of him,
> and the son of man that thou dost care for him? (Ps 8:5—RSV).

> But let thy hand be upon the man of thy right hand,
> the son of man whom thou has made strong for thyself!
> (Ps 80:17—RSV).

> I, I am he that comforts you;
> who are you that you are afraid of man who dies,
> of the son of man who is made like grass . . . . (Isa 51:12—RSV).

> How much less man, who is a maggot,
> and the son of man, who is a worm! (Job 25:6—RSV).[8]

In the Book of Ezekiel, it is found 93 times, and is God's favorite expression for designating the prophet. Some commentators argue that the phrase emphasizes Ezekiel's special

---

[7]Marshall, op.cit. 350.

[8]It should be noted that in the NRSV *ben-adam* (son of man) in all four of the preceding quotations is rendered as "mortal" or "human being." The reason for this would seemingly be the fact that the term "son of man" has, since New Testament times, acquired certain connotations that would not have been present at the time the above texts were written, so that the translation "mortal" or "human being" is, in fact, a more accurate rendering of the intention of the authors.

relationship with God, his special *messenger* status; others, on the contrary, would argue that it emphasizes his very ordinary status as a mere man in the presence of the Almighty. The NRSV translates the original Hebrew *ben'adam* with the word "mortal."

There is some justification for believing that on occasion Jesus himself may have used the phrase in this sense, i.e., as a substitute for "I."[9] For example in Luke's Gospel we read:

> For John the Baptist has come eating no bread and drinking no wine, and you say, "He has a demon"; the Son of Man has come eating and drinking, and you say, "Look, a glutton and a drunkard, a friend of tax collectors and sinners!" (7:33-34).

If Jesus did use this circumlocution for "I" sometimes, then it follows that "its titular use would not in every instance be inescapably present to Jesus' hearers. 'Son of Man' was thus a perfect vehicle for expressing the divine self-consciousness of Jesus while at the same time preserving the secrecy of his self-revelation from those who had blinded their eyes and closed their ears."[10]

Also, Jesus, by applying it to himself underlines his solidarity with the rest of the human race, and with the fallen human condition. He has come to identify himself with us, share our lot here on earth, from within. He takes upon himself a full human life, grounded in a specific culture, at a specific place and time in history. He is not suprahistorical in this sense. Sometimes Jesus is mistakenly presented as being above and outside history, a man of all times and places. Jesus may indeed be a man *for* all seasons, a man for all times and cultures, but this is not to deny that he was a man *of* his time and place in the same way as any other human being belongs to their time and place. We do not thereby imply that he accepted all that he found uncritically: on the contrary. But it does mean that

[9]See, for example, G. Vermes, *Jesus the Jew: A Historian's Reading of the Gospels* (London: Collins, 1973) 180–6.

[10]Idem. 350–1.

as a fully human being, he was rooted in history. We must be
ever alert to the temptation to deny full humanity to Jesus. As
John Macquarrie has pointed out, Jesus "differs from other
human beings in degree, not in kind."[11]

I think this is important for understanding and appreciating the mission of Jesus, and therefore for understanding and
appreciating the mission of the Church. Just as Jesus identified
with a specific culture, was rooted in it, and as such carried
out his mission of salvation, so likewise the Church must
become identified with each and every culture throughout
the world, must become rooted in them. And like Jesus this
demands that her approach must be both humble and willing
to serve. Any sense of cultural domination is detrimental to
the true work of evangelization. How can the missionary
understand a people, a culture, if he/she *overstands* it, looks
down on it, despises it or rejects it? That is not the way of the
Son of Man.

One of the tremendous gifts of the Spirit to the Church
in modern times is the growing awareness of the danger of
ethnocentrism, of seeing and judging all things from one
ethnic/cultural standpoint. To love our neighbor as ourselves,
is to love the whole person, in his or her cultural manifestation. Again, this does not mean that we have to abandon our
critical reason, but it does mean that our critical reason must
be enlightened by the Gospel, imbued with true Gospel values.
It means that we be ever ready to denounce all that would diminish the human person, or prevent growth, and at the same
time ever ready to promote all that is good, all that is positive,
all that is conducive to true personhood. It is for this reason
that we must examine carefully in the light of the Gospel all
that we find, rejecting nothing that is of value in all that different cultures to be found throughout the whole world.

In this context we are reminded once again of the centrality
of Christ in the whole plan of creation. All that has been created

---

[11]John Macquarrie, *Jesus Christ in Modern Thought* (London and
Philadelphia: SCM and Trinity Press International, 1990) 359. For a full
discussion of the humanity of Christ, see chapter 17.

is "in Christ" and "in view of Christ." This is an important point, because so often we are tempted to see Christ merely in terms of the response of God to the sin of Adam. But Christ is before Adam and superior to Adam and his significance is not dependent on Adam's sin, but on the contrary, infinitely surpasses it. The whole history of mankind is a history of salvation, a salvation that is always "in Christ." Creation is not something that occurred only at the beginning of time, but rather something that forms as it were the ever present foundation upon which the history of humanity rests. Creation therefore can and must be seen as a past, present, and future reality. As has been pointed out by Mario Serentha,[12]

> "In the beginning" (cf. Gen. Jo.) does not mean "before" history, or simply at the commencement, but rather means the foundations, the ultimate dimensions of the history of salvation. In other words it has to do with the understanding of our history, not something outside of it, or before it.

The grace given to Adam at the dawn of history is none other than the "grace of Christ," because the God of Creation is at one and the same time the God of the Covenant. God has always wished to share his life with humanity, to enter into communion with each and every human being, and Christ is the final and supreme expression of the divine will. In Christ the eternal will of God is made manifest and realized.

This also has the virtue of reminding us once again, that salvation is not merely negative in the sense of salvation *from*—it is also, and primarily, something positive in the sense of salvation *for,* and this aspect of salvation has been present right from the very beginning of God's plan. God's fundamental plan was that creation should share in his own happiness, his own life, and this fundamental plan was not changed because of humanity's sin. The goal or destiny of human beings

---

[12]Mario Serentha, *Gesu' Cristo Ieri, Oggi e Sempre. Saggio di cristologia,* 3rd. ed. (Torino: Elle Di Ci, 1988) 346.

remained the same after the fall as before the fall: participation, communion, sharing in the life of God.

Jesus' use of the title "Son of Man" as a self-designation reminds us of his complete solidarity with all of humanity, and therefore with all of creation. This is another way that we discover the universal significance of Jesus Christ.

Having said this, however, there are strong arguments for claiming that Jesus used it not just as a mere synonym for "I," but that through it he wished to underline that his presence with us is precisely a presence of humble service:

> For the Son of Man also came not to be served but to serve, and to give his life a ransom for many (Mark 10:45).

> Foxes have holes and birds of the air have nests; but the Son of Man has nowhere to lay his head (Luke 9:58).

Jesus comes to the world as one who serves, identifies himself with the human race in its fallen condition. This leads us into the second way in which Jesus uses the term Son of Man.

The Suffering Son of Man

This use of the title underlines the fact that Jesus conceived his mission as one that led inevitably to suffering, to the cross: "And he began to teach them that the Son of man must suffer many things, and be rejected by the elders and the chief scribes, and be killed, and after three days rise again" (Mark 8:31).

It is probable that this verse, given the exactitude with which it describes the passion, death, and resurrection of Christ is a *vaticinium ex eventu*.[13] In the overall picture, however, it is probably based directly on a reference by Jesus that he understood his mission as involving suffering and even death. The prediction of suffering was there, even though the precise details may have been absent. Would the disciples have been so shocked by the passion and death if Christ had so clearly foretold the details to them?

[13]See Wilfrid Harrington, *Mark* (Wilmington: Glazier, 1979) 128f.

In the idea of the suffering Son of Man, it would seem that here two streams of tradition flowing from the Old Testament—the Son of Man from Daniel 7 and that of the mysterious figure of the Suffering Servant from Isaiah 52 and 53—come together. All the suffering and trials of God's messengers who had gone before him find expression once again in this, *the* Messenger of God. He is indeed the long awaited Messiah, but a Messiah that conceives his role in terms of humiliation and suffering. This may be the precise reason why Jesus preferred to use the title "Son of Man" as a self-designation, rather than the title "Messiah," which had become too distorted, too politicized in the expectations of the Jews.

Jesus realized that to be faithful to the Father meant that in many instances he was going to encounter opposition and persecution from the world about him, particularly the world where self-interests dominated, and that to be faithful to his Father's will meant indeed taking up the cross. This is brought out even further in the verses immediately following in the Lucan parallel passage:

> Then he said to them all, "If any want to become my followers, let them deny themselves and take up their cross daily and follow me. For those who want to save their life will lose it, and those who lose their life for my sake will save it" (Luke 9:23-24).

The evangelist Mark is deeply aware that suffering is an integral part of God's plan of salvation, and he insists upon it, (9:9, 31; 10:23, 45; 12:31; 14:21) although balancing it with the image of the Son of Man in glory (9:9, 31; 10:23, 45; 12:31; 14:21). In order to arrive at the latter, he must pass through the former:

> For the Son of Man also came not to be served but to serve, and to give his life as a ransom for many (10:45).

This verse might be seen as a summary of Mark's Christology. It is sometimes disputed that this is an authentic phrase of the Lord's and its origin is to be sought in the early Church. Even if this is so, it still does not take away from the fact that

Jesus wished to underline that our dignity as members of God's family does not exempt us from service on behalf of our brothers and sisters. The theme of the suffering Son of Man once again upturns our human way of looking at reality, our human way of thinking how God "should" act. Very often we have preconceived ideas of how the Incarnate God should think and feel and relate to people, and these ideas come between us and how in fact God does think, feel, and act.

It was extremely difficult for the early Church—represented by Peter—to accept the scandal of the cross and suffering, to accept a suffering Messiah (It must have sounded to them like a contradiction in terms!) and yet they gradually realized that it is precisely here that God's love for humanity is shown in all its wonder and depth. To see the suffering of the Messiah in terms of the Father's will must have sounded blasphemous, but to see it in terms of God's entering into our life, sharing our existence, in terms of his love for us, must then and now be seen in all its wonder. God in Jesus takes upon himself our existential situation, our fallen condition, and in this wondrous way salvation comes to all humanity. Here we discover the innermost being of God as love. The image of the suffering Son of Man is one that encourages Christians in their daily struggles, pointing out that the glorified One is also the One who suffered on the cross.

The Eschatological Judge in Glory

In the Jewish tradition, at the time of Jesus, it would appear that this was the more common understanding of the phrase Son of Man. In Daniel 7:13 there is described a vision of the one coming "like a son of man" (RSV, NRSV has "human being"), and "to him was given dominion and glory and kingship" (v. 14). By the time of Jesus, this mysterious figure was, according to Cullmann, "generally thought of as an individual figure."[14] He was understood as a heavenly figure

---

[14]Cullman, *Christology*, 140.

who will come at the end of the world as the Judge of humanity.[15] Whether Jesus consciously applied this meaning to himself is a question for discussion,[16] but the fact is that the early Church did so. It is possible that this development occurred as a direct result of their experience of the resurrection.[17] Perhaps the best known and clearest expression of the eschatological use of the title Son of Man is found in Matthew's Gospel. For example in 24:30 we read: "Then the sign of the Son of Man will appear in heaven, and then all the tribes of the earth will mourn, and they will see the Son of Man coming on the clouds of heaven with power and great glory."

The aspect of judgment is found clearly in 19:28

> Jesus said to them, "Truly I tell you, at the renewal of all things, when the Son of Man is seated on the throne of his glory, you who have followed me will also sit on twelve thrones, judging the twelve tribes of Israel."

as also in 16:27

> For the Son of Man is to come with his angels in the glory of his Father, and then he will repay everyone for what he has done. Truly, I tell you, there are some standing here who will not taste death before they see the Son of Man coming in his kingdom.

[15]See R. H. Fuller, *The Foundations of New Testament Christology* (New York: Scribner's, 1965) 34–43.

[16]Bultmann regards the identification of Jesus with the eschatological Son of Man as a creation of the Church (see his *Theology of the New Testament*, 28–32). H. Gonzelman would agree: "In every case (i.e., of the use of the term "Son of Man") we have formulations of community doctrine" (*An Outline of the Theology of the New Testament* [New York, 1969, 134]). Oscar Cullmann (*Christology*, 156) maintains, however, that this position raises more problems than it solves.

[17]William O. Walker, "The Son of Man: Some Recent Developments" *CBQ* 45, (1983) 584–607, makes the interesting observation that "the origin of the Son of Man christology can be traced to a secondary

When Jesus was being questioned by the high priest during the trial, he was asked directly if he was "the Christ, the Son of God?" He answered with the words:

> You have said so. But I tell you,
> From now on you will see the Son of Man
> seated at the right hand of Power
> and coming on the clouds of heaven (Matt 26:64).

All of these quotations communicate the idea that the title "Son of Man" referred to the supreme role of Christ at the end of time. Both Mark and Luke make the same point:

> Those who are ashamed of me and of my words in this adulterous and sinful generation, of them the Son of Man will also be ashamed when he comes in the glory of his Father (Mark 8:38).

> Then he said to the disciples, "The days are coming when you will long to see one of the days of the Son of Man, and you will not see it. They will say to you, 'Look there!' or 'Look here!' Do not go, do not set off in pursuit. For as the lightning flashes and lights up the sky from one side to the other, so will the Son of Man be in his day" (Luke 17:22-24).

The early Church had a clear understanding that Christ, the Risen Lord would be there united with his Father on Judgement Day and that we would have to appear before him: "For all of us must appear before the judgment seat of

---

Christian exegetical tradition in which the initial interpretation of the resurrection on the basis of Ps 110:1 was expanded by the use of Dan 7:13, with the result that the resurrection was then seen as Jesus' Ascension to God as *Son of Man*. Thus the concept of Jesus as Son of Man originated within the exegetical tradition of the early Church, and it represented a secondary, not the primary, development within this tradition" (596–7). Later in the same essay he writes: "In any case, what is apparently reflected here is the tendency, which can be observed elsewhere, to project back into the lifetime of Jesus the attributes and status originally believed to have become his only after the resurrection (or perhaps not to become his until the *parousia*" (601).

Christ, so that each one may receive recompense for what has been done in the body, whether good or evil" (2 Cor 5:10; cf. 1 Cor 4:5). Christ was known as the "righteous judge" (2 Tim 4:8) who will eventually return to judge "the living and the dead."

John has no doubt about why Jesus is to be the eschatological judge—it is because he is the Son of Man:

> Very truly, I tell you, the hour is coming, and is now here, when the dead will hear the voice of the Son of God, and those who hear will live. For just as the Father has life in himself, so he has granted the Son also to have life in himself; and he has given him authority to execute judgment, because he is the Son of Man (5:25-27).

All of this throws tremendous light on our understanding of who Jesus is and what he means for us both now and later. He is the ever present Judge, a Judge of compassion and love, a Judge of forgiveness and mercy, but at the same time a Judge; and the criterion of judgment is the relation of the individual to Christ himself, a relationship that is actualized precisely in our relation to other people. Why? Because in him all other human beings are present so our relation to others is what defines our relation to him. Matthew in his description of the day of judgment brings this out clearly:

> When the Son of Man comes in his glory, and all the angels with him, then he will sit on the throne of his glory. All the nations will be gathered before him, and he will separate people one from another as a shepherd separates the sheep from the goats . . . . Truly, I tell you, just as you did it to one of the least of these who are members of my family, you did it to me (25:31-46).

Our eternal salvation or damnation is dependent on our relation to other people, on the measure with which we love them. And what greater love can we have for people than to communicate to them the Good News of Jesus Christ? To let the Spirit of God continue the mission of Christ through our lives, to let the Spirit of Christ become transparent in our lives—that is the mission of the Church and of each individual Christian.

It was the experience of the resurrection, experience of the action of the Risen Lord in their lives, that led the early Christians to see in the man Jesus the eschatological Son of Man, that enabled them to discover that in him all human beings were/are present. At the same time each person is invited to recognize and accept that connection by recognizing and accepting the road to full manhood and womanhood—the road traced out by Jesus, son of Mary and Son of God. And this brings us to the final aspect of the Son of Man title.

The One in Whom Humanity and Divinity Meet

Perhaps in no other title are the two aspects of the full humanity and full divinity of Jesus Christ so clearly intertwined. His utter solidarity with us in humanity, in our relationship to Adam, is fully affirmed and at the same time his utter solidarity with God in Glory and as Judge is maintained. Here we are in contact with the deepest stream of earliest Christology. It is also the most complete expression of the mission of the Son of Man—to bring each and every human being into the life that he has now. All human beings, descendants of Adam, share in Adam's fall, in the consequences of that fall—alienation in relationships, in the relationship with creation (especially that part of creation which is one's own body), alienation from other human beings, and alienation from God. Because of Christ people can now overcome that fundamental alienation in the very core of their existence, can once again find themselves and their destiny.

As in all the other titles, we see how this one too, applied to Jesus, acquired a totally new dimension and depth. At one and the same time we find united the concepts of humiliation and glorification, suffering and peace, death and life. All find their unity in the one person, Jesus of Nazareth. The Son of Man is also the Son of God, and the early Church saw this connection. For example, in Matthew we read: "For the

Son of Man is to come with his angels in the glory of his Father . . . ." (16:27).

We find the same trend in John 5:25-27 where the two phrases "Son of God" and "Son of man" are used interchangeably. Another example is 1 Thessalonians 1:10, where we find a reference to the "Son from heaven" where we would have expected the phrase "Son of Man." This was probably due to the fact that for Gentile readers the phrase "Son of Man" would be unintelligible, or confusing. And as we mentioned earlier this is also the probable reason why the title "Son of Man" tended to fade out of use as the Church extended its boundaries more and more into the Gentile world. Furthermore, as I. H. Marshall has pointed out, the fact that it was dropped by the early Church, was presumably

> because of its unsuitability to express the fullness of the Church's belief about Jesus and especially because of its peculiarity in Greek translation. It was now possible to use the title "Son of God" without restraint as the term best fitted to express the supreme place occupied by Jesus.[18]

As another commentator has pointed out, "the public proclamation of Jesus as Son of God belongs to the mission of the postresurrection church."[19]

Once again we come face to face with the profound mystery of Jesus Christ—the mystery that in this man God was totally present and active. Chalcedon tried to express this insight in metaphysical categories saying that in him there were two "natures," human and divine, united in one *hypostasis,* united in one personal relationship that is the second Person of the Blessed Trinity. We may have difficulty with the *words* that Chalcedon used, but the whole New Testament testifies to the *reality* they tried to capture and pin down. In Jesus Christ we find our own humanity, our weakness, our struggle, our

[18]I. H. Marshall, "The Synoptic Son of Man . . . " 351.
[19]Darrell J. Doughty, "The Authority of the Son of Man" in *Zeitschrift Für Die Neuntestamentliche Wissenschaft* 74 (1983) 181n.

temptation, and at the same time we find God, God's love, God's compassion, God's mercy and forgiveness. God the Father alone can be the author of our salvation and in Jesus Christ we meet the fullness of God. For that reason all human beings can find in Jesus and his Spirit salvation and only there. The two great theologians of the New Testament sum it up in these words:

> If the Spirit of him who raised Jesus from the dead dwells in you, he who raised Christ from the dead will give life to your mortal bodies also through his Spirit that dwells in you (Rom 8:11).

> And this is eternal life, that they may know you, the only true God, and Jesus Christ whom you have sent (John 17:3).

CHAPTER 7

Christ, the Crucified and Risen One

When the aged Simeon held the Christ child in his arms, he gave thanks to the Almighty for having granted him the privilege of seeing "The salvation of God." Inspired by the Spirit, the old man was able to see beyond the weakness of the helpless babe and in faith discern the presence of the One who saves. Salvation is not a thing but a person, not an action so much as an encounter, not a business so much as a relationship. Jesus in his very being is the salvation of God—the salvation, that life of blessedness, into which each and every human being is called. Salvation is nothing less than to enter into divine life by means of Christ and his Spirit.

The revelation of that salvation achieved its most perfect expression in the life, death, and resurrection of Jesus Christ in his paschal mystery. It is important that the whole mystery be taken into account and its unity be maintained, and that includes his passion and death.[1] Death is not just the last moment of a life, but rather gathers that life together. From the moment of our birth death is our constant companion, and as Karl Rahner has pointed out, "In the Christian idea of freedom, the one free act in human life which is ultimately

---

[1] In this connection, see Dermot A. Lane, *Christ at the Center* (New York: Paulist, 1991) especially chapters 3 and 4.

decisive occurs only through actual death, and not independent of it."[2] Death is the moment in which the decision of our life on earth receives its definitive expression and its unalterable seal. It stamps our life in a radically definitive way.

The life of Jesus in its totality found its culmination and recapitulation on the cross. His words, "Father, into your hands I commend my Spirit" (Luke 23:46), could be an apt description not only of death, but also of his whole life. His entering into God's realm of thought, action, relationships, his radical trust in his Father—all that which he lived out in his thirty-three years on earth—find their highest expression on Calvary. Indeed, it is only in death that they *could* find their definitive expression. Without his death, his life would not be definitive or sealed; it would not be complete.

Throughout his life he demonstrated and taught that God's ways are not our ways, that they are indeed radically different, and it is on the Cross that all human ways of thinking and judging are overturned and God's power and strength and love are revealed in an unimaginable new way. The cross of Christ is the radical revelation of how God the Father relates to us. He is not the God of the Greeks, distant, untouched and untouchable, incapable of being effected in any way by his creation, but rather God who in some altogether mysterious way can suffer with humanity, can identify with our situation here below, and who is prepared to go to any length to show his care for us, his forgiveness, his love. On the cross we see the radical nature of the revelation of Jesus Christ as Emmanuel, "God-with-us." For that reason the great St. Paul knew that the essence of his preaching was the Cross of Christ:

> Where is the one who is wise? Where is the scribe? Where is the debater of this age? Has not God made foolish the wisdom of the world? For since, in the wisdom of God, the world did

[2]Karl Rahner and Wilhelm Thusing, "The Death of Jesus and the Finality of Revelation" in *A New Christology* (New York: Seabury, 1980) 38.

not know God through wisdom, God decided, through the foolishness of our proclamation, to save those who believe. For Jews demand signs and Greeks desire wisdom, but we proclaim Christ crucified, a stumbling block to Jews and foolishness to Gentiles (1 Cor 1:20-24).

God's wisdom and power receive their supreme revelation on the Cross. How scandalous! How startling! We can forget it so easily, forget that in the Cross the God of our Christian faith receives his most supreme revelation to humanity. The Cross is what puts such profound content into the phrase, "God is love"; the Cross is what gives tremendous significance to the words "God forgives us"; the Cross is what explains the words, "God is our Father"; the Cross is what underpins the phrase, "God is our Savior." The Cross is what tells us what faith, hope and love are all about, what relationships are all about. The Cross, which to the Romans was a sign of disgrace, dishonor, shame, humiliation, and degradation, has become for us Christians the sign also of what is grace, honor, exaltation, hope, and love.

At the same time it is likewise true that the Cross reveals to us our own fallen situation, our own lack of salvation, our own need, the depth of our capacity for evil, darkness, and sin. But the paradox is that precisely there where we discover our own need of salvation is where God comes to us as our Savior. The Cross is the supreme exemplar of that paradox which we find at the heart of the message of Christ, that paradox that tells us that only by losing our life can we find it, that only by dying can we live.

This brings us to the other aspect of the mystery, the resurrection. The Cross of Christ, to be fully understood, needs the witness of the resurrection. The two form a unity; in isolation the correct understanding of each aspect is impossible. St. John, in trying to bring out this fundamental unity, chose the one phrase "raised up" to capture the twofold aspect of the mystery. The Cross is the bond which unites the Jesus of history and the Christ of faith. Jurgen Moltmann has put it like this:

The point at which the history of Jesus and the proclamation of Christ coincide is the cross on Golgotha. In the light of Jesus' life his death is the end of his messianic mission. In the light of his resurrection, however, his death is his true beginning and the beginning of the Kingdom of God on earth.[3]

Prior to the resurrection the message of his life and death was not clear. What did Jesus mean when he said, "I came that they may have life and have it abundantly" (John 10:10), if all the time the threat of death hung suspended above, not only our heads, but above his own head? For death seems to negate all one's striving, all one's hope and deepest longings, all that one is and has. Without the resurrection death would have had the final word, and our hope would have no solid foundation. For that reason the resurrection is absolutely central for the understanding of the crucified Christ as the Savior of the world. Without the resurrection our faith would be without adequate support, something vain and empty.

In the Paschal mystery we discover to what a profound extent God the Father has committed himself to humanity, and to its welfare, for the resurrection is as it were the Father's response to the Cross, God's own response to the love revealed therein. There we see how radically real is promise of the Book of Revelation:

> See, the home of God is among mortals,
> He will dwell with them as their God;
> they will be his peoples,
> and God himself will be with them (21:3).

It is not just a beautiful metaphor, a powerful image to help our spirituality, but is real in the realest possible way. The Good News that comes from the Father is not something exterior to him, something outside himself, not a mere verbal promise no matter how wonderful that may be, but is nothing less than Godself. When God the Father com-

---

[3] *Theology Today* (London and Philadelphia: SAM Press and Trinity Press International, 1988) 38.

municates himself in love there are no half measures—he communicates *GODSELF,* and the wonderful mystery of the resurrection of Jesus Christ is the greatest expression of God's universal salvific will and God's universal salvific power. The resurrection is the powerful light at the heart of the Gospel message, the light which illumines all that went before it, giving it meaning and significance, and all that follows it. The resurrection was the confirmation of all that Jesus had taught and the manifestation of God the Father's self-communication to humanity. For that reason the paschal mystery in all its multifaceted unity is the central master key which enables us to enter into all the other aspects of salvation and to savor them.

It is important to recall that the New Testament was written after the early Church had lived out their faith in the resurrection for a number of years. The New Testament is a collection of theological documents arising out of the faith experience of the early Christian communities. This experience had had a profound effect on their lives and on their understanding of Jesus the Nazarene. Their experience of the resurrection was understood as the decisive vindication of all that Jesus had said and done. The first community of Christians experienced Jesus as alive, as with them, as risen. Because of the resurrection the full significance of the salvific quality of Jesus' life and death was revealed. That is why the life, death, and resurrection form one indissoluble mystery. To separate the Cross from the resurrection is to misunderstand both. The Cross without the resurrection is just another sad event in humankind's long litany of sorrows; the resurrection without the death is meaningless for us, for without it Christ would not have identified with our most profound experience of alienation, would not have completed his own life, and so salvation would be something outside our experience, outside the human reality. Likewise to exalt the resurrection at the expense of the Cross can be an escapism from the present reality, escapism from the daily struggle to live out our Christianity here below. The fight is not yet over, even though the definitive battle has been fought and won. Christ continues to fight in and through the Church until the moment when he will be "all in all."

Each local church would give a particular nuance to the description of the resurrection tradition, and so each of the documents of the New Testament reflects the particular light of its origin, the particular hue as it were of the dazzling light of the risen Lord who had been crucified on Calvary. The peculiarity of each document arises in part from the specific peculiarity by each community or individual of the experience of the Risen Lord in their midst.

It is important to insist on the priority of the experience of the Lord as risen. Karl Rahner writes:

> We can admit without any qualms that the reports which are presented to us at first glance as historical details of the event of the resurrection or of the appearances cannot be harmonized completely. Hence they are to be explained as secondary literary and dramatic embellishments of the original experience that "Jesus is alive," rather than as descriptions of the experience itself in its real and original nature. So far as the nature of this experience is accessible to us, it is to be explained after the manner of our experience of the powerful Spirit of the living Lord rather than in a way which either likens this experience too closely to mystical visions of an imaginative kind in later times, or understands it as an almost physical sense experience. There is no such sense experience of someone who has really reached fulfillment, even presupposing that he must indeed have freely "manifested" himself.[4]

The faith of the early Church finds its basis in this experience itself, rather than the empty tomb, or even the resurrection appearances.

The death of Christ must have posed a tremendous problem for the early Church. They looked to their past and found a clue in the treatment of the prophets—but all of this had to be within the saving plan of God. Thus we find in Acts:

---

[4]Karl Rahner, *Foundations of Christian Faith* (New York: Crossroad, 1978) 276.

This man, handed over to you according to the definite plan and foreknowledge of God, you crucified and killed by the hands of those outside the law. But God raised him up, having freed him from death, because it was impossible for him to be held in its power (2:23-24).

The death of Jesus could only be understood in terms of the loving, saving plan of God. Anything else would be offensive to the God revealed by Jesus Himself. In this connection Wolfhart Pannenberg has written:

> From the perspective of the Scriptures, the disciples sought to find not only the necessity for Jesus' having to follow the way of the cross but also the meaning of this event. Thereby it seems that the notion that Jesus did not die for himself but for us had already taken on a fundamental importance. Jesus' resurrection had proved that he though innocent had been rejected, given over to the Romans and executed. Thus the meaning of his death could only be understood as an expression of service to humanity in the name of the love of God revealed in his message, which determined his whole mission.[5]

Likewise it must be recalled that for the early Christians the resurrection was and always will be first and foremost a mystery of faith. It was the supreme intervention of God in history, something radically different from all other miracles. In recent decades much has been written about the "historicity" of the resurrection, as if the resurrection was an event in time and space just as, for example, one might question the historicity of the return to life of Lazarus, or the widow of Nain's son. The resurrection of Jesus Christ from the dead was not an event of the same order as those other two, it was not the mere resuscitation of a corpse, but was and is something radically new, something that transcends the categories of space and time, and therefore transcends the strictly historical. As the Pontifical Biblical Commission put it, the resurrection of Christ

---

[5]Wolfhart Pannenberg, *Jesus—God and Man* (Philadelphia: Westminster, 1968) 247.

cannot be proved in an empirical way. For by it Jesus is introduced into "the world to come." This can, indeed, be deduced as a reality from the appearances of Christ in glory to certain preordained witnesses, and it is corroborated by the fact that Jesus' tomb was found open and empty. But one may not simplify this question excessively, as if any historian, making use only of scientific investigation, could prove it with certainty as a fact accessible to any observer whatsoever. In this matter there is also needed "the decision of faith," or better "an open heart," so that the mind may be moved to assent.[6]

This is not to say that it is unhistorical but that our understanding of the merely "historical" is incapable of encompassing it.[7] The resurrection is the passing of Jesus through death to the utterly new, utterly transformed, definitive life. This passage of Jesus gave to the disciples a whole new lens with which to view the Jesus who had walked the roads of Palestine with them. We have to distinguish between the manner in which Jesus appeared to his disciples while he was with them in his earthly life, and the manner in which they understood him when they experienced him as the Risen One, the one who now lives. In the resurrection God the Father revealed to the disciples, and through them to us, the ultimate meaning of creation and of his plan of salvation. God the Father in the resurrection proclaims the ultimate triumph of good over evil, of justice over injustice, of life over death.

[6]Joseph A. Fitzmyer, *Scripture & Christology. A Statement of the Biblical Commission with a Commentary* (New York: Paulist, 1986) 24.

[7]In this regard it can be helpful to keep in mind the distinction which many modern German theologians make between *Historie,* i.e., historical understanding that is based on empirical facts gained from a study of documents and which seeks to express the causal connections involved in human affairs; *Geschichte,* which refers more to the event itself, seen as an encounter or *happening* between human beings; and *Heilgeschichte* (Salvation history), which refers to the encounter between God and human beings, to the experience itself, and which implies an understanding of it that has been mediated by faith. The resurrection would therefore be understood as *Heilgeschichte* rather than as *Historie.*

While remembering what we have said about the priority of the first Christians' experience of Jesus as alive, as risen, it must be admitted that that experience cannot be separated from how they interpreted, and indeed the interpretation enters as it were into the experience.[8] For that reason it is important to look even though very briefly at how the Church tried to present and interpret that experience of resurrection as it is found in the New Testament.[9]

Paul is the earliest writer of the New Testament corpus, and throughout his writings he maintains the unity between the passion, death, and resurrection. They are not to be separated. Indeed, in reading Paul's Letters one is struck by the almost total neglect of the life of Christ before his passion. He focuses in on the climax. The Good News is that the crucified One has been raised from the dead. He is now the Lord of creation and the source of all salvation. In Paul we discover above all the impossibility of separating soteriology from Christology. The kernel of the Good News is expressed by Paul in many passages, but chapter 15 of his First Letter to the Corinthians is of particular significance. There Paul, quoting what was probably the oldest "Creed" of the Church, expresses in formal terms the tradition, the *paradosis* of the very first Christian communities:

> For I handed on to you as of first importance what I in turn had received: that Christ died for our sins in accordance with the scriptures, and that he was buried, and that he was raised on the third day in accordance with the scriptures, and that he appeared to Cephas, then to the twelve (vv. 3-5).

[8] In this connection, see the remarks of Francis Schuessler Fiorenza in his *Foundational Theology* (New York: Crossroad, 1992) 40–42.

[9] For an overall view of the Resurrection see, G. O'Collins, *The Resurrection of Christ* (Valley Forge, Pa., 1974); also his, *Interpreting the Resurrection* (New York: Paulist, 1988). For a short outline and bibliography on the subject, see Raymond E. Brown, Joseph A. Fitzmyer, and Roland E. Murphy, eds., *The New Jerome Biblical Commentary* (Englewood Cliffs, N.J.: Prentice Hall, 1990, 1968) 1373-7.

Christ died and was buried—burial for the Jews was the final, definitive stage in the death process. There is no doubt about Christ's taking to himself our death in all its seeming finality, all its seeming negation of life's aspirations and desires. God raised up Christ on the third day—for Paul, the resurrection is always the action of God, he is its agent—and he appeared to many. The appearances are important for the authentication of the resurrection. It is interesting to note that Paul places his own experience of the risen Lord on the road to Damascus on the same level as the other appearances: "Last of all, as to one untimely born, he appeared also to me" (v. 8). In this way he underlines the relationship between the resurrection and his apostolic activity, for it is the former that gives the latter its foundation and authority.

Because of his experience of the resurrection, he must proclaim the Good News. He realizes that because Christ is now risen, then a new and wonderful message of hope has broken in on world history, a message of hope that is for all humanity without exception, and that all humanity has the right to hear it, and that God has commissioned him, Paul, to carry that message to others, to bring the Good News of salvation—made concrete in the resurrection, to all his brothers and sisters. Each human being called into existence by God is called ultimately to be what Christ is now. Christ is the "first fruits" (v. 20), the concrete promise of the final harvest. For that reason the Gospel message is the "power to save" (Rom 1:16). The early Church had no hesitation in proclaiming the fullness of the humanity of Christ, and that the resurrection was the "resurrection of the body." This is essential if the resurrection is to be "good news" *for us,* if it is to be truly *salvific.* The resurrection underlines that God comes to us as our Savior. The risen Christ brings humanity to its perfection and happiness in the very life of God. In the resurrection the salvation of all humanity and all history is proclaimed in a definitive and irrevocable manner. Because of the resurrection, Jesus the Proclaimer becomes the proclaimed. For that reason it is a powerful instrument of hope, a powerful dynamo of energy in the building of a better world despite at times the apparent uselessness of it all, despite the paradox of death.

In order to help the faith of the Corinthians in the resurrection—and Paul has no doubt that the resurrection is founded on faith, not on empirical data—he invokes the example of the seed. Who could imagine that from a tiny seed a great tree could grow? Could one who had never seen the mighty oak possibly imagine it from the tiny seed resting in the palm of one's hand? And yet, that seed must die in order that the final tree can be born (vv. 35-58. Cf. John 12:24). The death-life process within creation is an analogy of the Paschal Mystery.

And Paul makes it clear that the whole person, body and soul, is to share in the resurrection. The human being is a psychosomatic unity, and it is this unity that is called to share in the life of the risen Lord. The body is not to be sacrificed to the spirit. The human person will be transformed, what was perishable will become imperishable, what was inglorious will become glorious, what was weak will become full of power, what was physical will become spiritual—i.e., Spirit filled. The change effected by the resurrection in the body of the Lord, was a change from corruptibility to incorruptibility, from passability to impassibility, from mortality to immortality. We need a body to be fully human, but what precise type of body is another question. The resurrection is a new creation, something that is beyond the capacity of our imagination. And so Paul concludes with a quotation from Hosea 13:14:

> Where, O Death, is your victory?
> Where, O death, is your sting? (v. 55)

Death has not disappeared from the human scene; but its ultimacy has, and for that reason it cannot be victorious, it cannot have the last word, and so its "sting" has been drained off, has been removed.

The simple phrase "He is risen" is what gives us hope despite the signs of death all around us. Everywhere we look we see death, the death of the innocent hungry children in Ethiopia, the death arising out of senseless war and guerilla battles, the death from cancer in the hospitals of the world, the deaths of our own loved ones, the death in our own selves, in our inter-personal relations. But despite all that we can still hope, still find meaning, still continue striving for a better world, continue striving for greater justice and peace, equality and brother-hood. That is why the power of the resurrection is a present power. "He is risen" proclaims his living presence with us *now*, a presence that is life-giving, that is full of promise, and a promise that is sure.

Because he is risen the mystery of suffering is accepted, or at least made habitable. His resurrection enables us to believe that all the countless crosses of humanity are somehow caught up in the mystery of salvation, caught up in God's plan of love—that they too are part of that mystery which culminates in the resurrection. The resurrection is not "pie in the sky" but a powerful force now operative in the world to bring about its salvation. It is not to turn us away from this world, but to love it as God loves it. It was for this world that Christ died and rose again, it was for us here and now. A true under-standing and appreciation of the resurrection should not lead us to try and escape from this world, but rather should lead us into an ever deeper relationship with it, knowing that it is indeed the object of God's eternal love, and that it is destined to fullness—a fullness to which the Church has been called to witness and to collaborate in bringing it about.

It is Paul's faith in the resurrection that enables him to develop his profound understanding of the person and work of Christ, his Christology. This is expressed in many passages, but two in particular stand out. The first is the famous Christological hymn from Colossians:

> He is the image of the invisible God, the firstborn of all crea-tion; for in him all things in heaven and on earth were created, things visible and invisible, whether thrones or dominions or rulers or powers—all things have been created through him and for him. He himself is before all things, and in him all things hold together. He is the head of the body, the church; he is the beginning, the firstborn from the dead, so that he might come to have first place in everything. For in him all the fullness of God was pleased to dwell, and through him God

was pleased to reconcile to himself all things, whether on earth or in heaven, by making peace through the blood of his cross (1:15-20).

The full significance of Christ is made possible through the passion-death-resurrection event. The risen Lord stands radiating light over all of history, revealing to us our origin and our destiny. Through him all humanity can achieve that same fullness, that same completeness represented by the resurrection. The second vital text is that of Philippians 2:5-11:

> Let the same mind be in you that was in Christ Jesus
>   who, though he was in the form of God,
>   did not regard equality with God
>   as something to be exploited,
> but emptied himself,
>   taking the form of a slave,
>   being born in human likeness.
> And being found in human form,
>   he humbled himself
>   and became obedient to the point of death—
>   even death on a cross.
>
> Therefore God also highly exalted him
>   and gave him the name
>   that is above every name,
> so that at the name of Jesus
>   every knee should bend,
>   in heaven and on earth and under the earth,
> and every tongue should confess
>   that Jesus Christ is Lord,
>   to the glory of God the Father.

God the Father responds to the Cross with the resurrection. The sacrifice of the Cross, Jesus of Nazareth stretched on the wooden altar of Calvary, is a sacrifice that belongs to all humanity, is accepted by the Father and because of it Christ, the new Adam, enters into glory, and so the salvation of humanity becomes a reality. In the risen Lord the salvation of each and every human being is made possible. He is the

Lord and Savior of all peoples. The resurrection is the ground of our hope.

For Matthew, Jesus is the new Moses, the deliverer and formator of a new people, the maker of a new covenant. Like all the evangelists Matthew is not clear on the details of the resurrection (could he be?), but what he does proclaim unhesitatingly is the reality of the resurrection, and this is placed on the lips of an angel to underline that it is a revelation of God:

> But the angel said to the women, "Do not be afraid; I know that you are looking for Jesus who was crucified. He is not here; for he has been raised, as he said. Come, see the place where he lay. Then go quickly and tell his disciples, 'he has been raised from the dead, and indeed he is going ahead of you to Galilee; there you will see him.' This is my message for you" (28:5-7).

Jesus has attained the fullness of life, and in him all humanity can now achieve it. His new life is now the inheritance of humanity, and the Church living in this new life, is the witness to it. The Church in and through her love of God and love of the neighbor testifies to the presence of the risen Lord in her midst. It is the resurrection that makes the Church possible and it is the resurrection that defines her mission. For that reason Matthew unites the two in the powerful closing sentence of his Gospel, the climax of all that he wished to communicate:

> And Jesus came and said to them, "All authority in heaven and on earth has been given to me. Go therefore and make disciples of all nations, baptizing them in the name of the Father and of the Son and of the Holy Spirit, and teaching them to obey everything that I have commanded you. And remember, I am with you always, to the end of the age" (28:18-20).

Jesus as the new Moses constitutes a new people and orders them to live a new kind of life, a life that is in accordance with all that he has taught, and one that is animated by none other than his own Spirit. The mission of the Church is to witness to this new life that has erupted on the world in the resurrection.

The evangelist Mark likewise concentrates on the empty tomb, especially if we accept 16:8 as the original ending of the Gospel. Again it is an angel, a messenger of God, who makes the announcement. The resurrection is first and foremost God's salvific dealing with Jesus, and through Jesus, with humanity as a whole:

> Do not be alarmed; you are looking for Jesus of Nazareth, who was crucified. He has been raised; he is not here. Look, there is the place they laid him (16:6).

The empty tomb is a powerful expression of the resurrection from a negative point of view. God is not to be found among the dead but among the living. Do not look for him in the tombs, in the cemeteries, but seek him in the crowded streets of our modern cities, seek him in the market places, seek him in the hub-bub of our interpersonal encounters. God the Father is not a God of death (such would be a direct contradiction of his first title "Father"!), but of life. Through the resurrection Jesus proclaims in an utterly definitive and dramatic way that he is life, that he can give life, that he is able to fulfill his claim: "I have come that they may have life and have it abundantly" (John 10:10). The tomb is a profound image of all that is negative, all that threatens a person's existence. The tomb conjures up images of darkness, enclosure, confinement, sadness, and death. Now the tomb is empty, the stone is rolled away, and so light breaks through, bonds are smashed, sadness and death dispelled, and joy reigns.

Again it is to be noted that in the second ending the theme of resurrection and mission is more strongly emphasized and more clearly enunciated:

> Later he appeared to the eleven themselves as they were sitting at the table; and he upbraided them for their lack of faith and stubbornness, because they had not believed those who saw him after he had risen. And he said to them, "Go into all the world and proclaim the good news to the whole creation" (16:14-15).

This is followed by the ascension (Mark presents it as taking place on Easter day). Understood theologically, the ascension is the completion of the resurrection—the "setting down at the right hand of God." Jesus is now in very truth "the Lord" and so he is called in the closing two verses of the Gospel:

> So then the Lord Jesus, after he had spoken to them, was taken up into heaven and sat down at the right hand of God. And they went out and proclaimed the good news everywhere, while the Lord worked with them and confirmed the message by the signs that accompanied it (16:19-20).

The theme of Jesus as Lord, the *Kyrios* is taken up by Luke in his two-volume work. The title *Kyrios* ("Lord") emphasized that the bearer had absolute authority over something or someone. On giving the title to Jesus, Luke is acknowledging that he is more than merely human—and that the resurrection proves that. The resurrection had clearly proclaimed Jesus as Lord (and Luke tends to reserve the use of that title until after the resurrection). The Crucified One has been raised up by God, all that he said and preached has been vindicated. Salvation is now a reality. As is the case with the other evangelists, Luke too describes the events surrounding the resurrection with amazing simplicity: He is risen.

> "Why do you look for the living among the dead? He is not here, but has risen. Remember how he told you, while he was still in Galilee, that the Son of Man must be handed over to sinners, and be crucified, and on the third day rise again" (24:6-7).

From the resurrection flows the mission of the Church and Luke dedicates his entire second volume, Acts, to it, which describes the foundation of mission, (the ascension, understood as the completion of the resurrection, and Pentecost, understood as the consequence of the resurrection); and the realization or actualization of it (first in Palestine, and then throughout the whole world). Because the Risen One now is Lord, and through him, and only through him, salvation is to be achieved, then he must be proclaimed:

There is salvation in no one else, for there is no other name under heaven given among mortals by which we must be saved (Acts 4:12).

God exalted him at his right hand as Leader and Savior that he might give repentance to Israel and forgiveness of sins (5:31).

This brings us to John's Gospel, written some decades after the other three. John unites very profoundly the two aspects of death and resurrection and the whole narrative constitutes the one story of Christ's glorification. Being raised up on the cross is the first movement of that process, the resurrection is the second movement completing it. His actual testimony to the resurrection is in full accord with the tradition.

The resurrection—which no one witnessed, in the literal sense of the term—is first reported by the women, one of whom was Mary Magdalene, who is mentioned in all the accounts. In our time the full significance of this is beginning to be seen. We are so accustomed to the importance of the apostolic witness that we forget that the first witnesses to the resurrection—not in the sense of being *eyewitnesses* to the event, but in the sense of being capacitated to testify to its reality—were the women, and that they were the first sent by the risen Lord to proclaim his resurrection to others. Mary Magdalene and the other women were the apostles to the apostles. In this touch, I think, we discover one of the hidden depths of the Gospel message still to be plumbed. The New Testament, while recognizing the importance of the testimony of the apostles, did not silence the obviously deep tradition of the place of women in witnessing to the resurrection.

The encounter of Mary Magdalene with the risen Lord is particularly instructive. In the brief exchange of the two names, "Mary," "Rabboni," we realize that death has been vanquished, its sting removed, and the loving interpersonal relationship established this side of the tomb has not been broken. On the contrary, the resurrection has given it the capacity to rise to a totally other plain, to be eternal. That is why Mary must let go of the old relationship in order to find it again, renewed and infinitely elevated. Prior to the resurrection all loving relationships were saddened by the ever present threat of death, now that threat has been transcended, and in faith we now know that love can indeed reign supreme, that joy and life and peace can truly be unending.

John brings his account of the resurrection, and of his whole Gospel, to its climax in the episode of the appearance of the risen Christ to the apostles with Thomas being present. The Synoptics had all mentioned the initial incredulity of the disciples in the resurrection, an incredulity that receives its maximum expression in Thomas. Now he, the one who has become synonymous with doubt, is the one who makes the most perfect affirmation of faith in the risen Lord: "My Lord and my God." John's Gospel opens with the words, "In the beginning was the Word, and the Word was with God, and the Word was God." With the proclamation of faith by Thomas, the full significance of the Jesus event is made clear. In Jesus Christ, the omnipotent, eternal God was present. The very "stuff" of God was in Jesus Christ. This is the infinite "more than" which is found in all the other titles. This is what made Jesus "more than" a prophet, "more than" a teacher, "more than" a king, "more than" an ambassador, "more than" a liberator, and this was the faith of the first Christians. And in case anyone should miss the significance of this we have the inspired words: "Blessed are those who have not seen and yet believe." It was this profound truth of the New Testament that the Council of Nicaea expressed in more theological language: Jesus Christ is "from the being/substance/*ousia* of the Father, God from God, Light from Light, true God from true God, begotten not made, one in being/substance/*homoousios* with the Father." The Word of God, the Gospel itself, is the saving power of God active in the world, the power that can transform the individual and the world in which he or she lives.

Proclamation of the Gospel is the ordinary means that God uses for bringing people into communion with Him, into salvation, and they become thereby the light of the world. The Word of God is the beginning of creation, the beginning of salvation and it is the Word who sustains that creation and that salvation, and who will finally bring all to fullness. We are called to be ministers, servants of that Word—and it is that same Word that empowers our message and empowers its reception in others. John concludes his Gospel with the words:

> But these are written so that you may come to believe that Jesus is the Messiah, the Son of God, and that through believing you may have life in his name (John 20:31).

The mission of the Church springs from the fact that all humanity has the right to that "life in his name." God calls all Christians to be the bearer of the light of the Risen Lord to the world. A Christian is therefore one commissioned by God to perform this service in and for the world. The symbol of this light is the bare Cross, which represents not just the death but also the resurrection. Paul reminds us:

> For the message about the cross is foolishness to those who are perishing, but to us who are being saved it is the power of God (1 Cor 1:18).

CHAPTER 8

Christ, Revealer and Sender of the Spirit

It is relatively easy to understand Jesus as revealer of the Father; it is a little more difficult to see him as revealer of the Spirit. Yet, precisely because the Spirit cannot be separated from the Father and the Son, Jesus is as much the revealer of the Spirit as he is of the Father, for as St. Paul reminds us, "in him the whole fullness of deity dwells bodily" (Col 2:9). This is a truth that must never be forgotten. Just as we cannot know the Father except through the Son, so likewise we cannot know the Spirit except through the same Son. Christology cannot be separated from pneumatology. As St. Basil (A.D. 329–379) wrote, "in all things the Spirit is inseparable and wholly incapable of being parted from the Father and the Son."[1]

One of the reasons for our difficulty in understanding the Spirit is our tendency to see the third Person of the Blessed Trinity in isolation, rather than in conjunction with the Father

---

[1] *On the Spirit, XVI. Nicene and Post-Nicene Fathers of the Christian Church,* 2nd Series, vol. VIII (Edinburgh: T & T Clark; Grand Rapids: Eerdmans, reprinted, 1989) 23.

and the Son. There is a tendency to see the Father as God before us, the Son as God for us, and the Holy Spirit as God with us. This may be helpful in some ways, but in other ways it is not helpful for it separates the three persons of the Blessed Trinity in their inner being and in their relation to us. But, as the earliest creeds of the Church make clear, the Spirit is active wherever and whenever the Father and Son are. The Spirit is proclaimed as "Lord and giver of life" just like the Father and the Son. By proclaiming the *lordship* of the Spirit, the Church proclaims the Spirit's full divinity. All creation and every blessing comes from God the Father, through the Son in the Spirit. And if the whole world is to become indeed a "sacrifice of praise" to God our heavenly Father, it can only become so in the Spirit and through the Son. The Holy Spirit is not just one spirit among others, but is "holy" precisely because the Spirit belongs to the eternal being of the divinity, belongs to the totally Other.

A second difficulty is that while the words "Father" and "Son" evoke human images for us, the word "Spirit" does not, for it is taken from natural phenomena, from the action of breathing, from the wind, and the symbols used to express the reality of the Spirit are likewise symbols taken from nature: water, fire, air. No doubt, this is providential, for with the word "Spirit" we are constantly reminded that God is absolute mystery, that God is the totally Other, and the danger of over anthropomorphizing God is thereby obviated.

Furthermore, just as the Spirit can only be understood in conjunction with the Father and the Son, so likewise the true meaning of the terms "Father" and "Son" applied to God can only be understood in terms of the Spirit. The Spirit is the Spirit of the Father in his fatherhood. In other words, the Father is understood precisely in the breathing forth, just as the same Spirit is the Spirit of the Son in his sonship, for the Son is understood as breathed forth. Between the Son and the Spirit there is absolute communion and unity in the plan of salvation. Together with the Father and the Son, the Holy Spirit is active in revealing to us God's wonderful design of the plan of salvation and in every aspect of its execution.

Like all of Christian revelation, the revelation of the Spirit is gradual and culminates in Jesus Christ.[2] According to all four evangelists Jesus is the bearer of the Spirit of God, *par excellence*. The whole life of the pre-resurrection Jesus can be seen as being filled with the Holy Spirit, and even though in Scripture the references to the Spirit are relatively few,[3] they are found in strategic places and are emphatic. Furthermore, it must be noted that while it is true that Jesus *speaks* directly about the Spirit very little, yet his entire life proclaims the *action* of the Spirit. Indeed all of Scripture speaks of the Spirit in terms of action, dynamism, and this alerts us to the "being" of the Spirit in the mystery of the Trinity. If it is proper to the Father to "beget," and proper to the Son to "be begotten," it is proper to the Spirit to "be begetting." To put it another way, if it is proper to the Father to love, and proper to the Son to be beloved, then it is proper to the Spirit to be love itself.

It is not surprising, therefore, that when we examine Scripture what we discover first is not what the Spirit is, but rather what the Spirit does in the life of Jesus and in the life of his disciples. In the references to the Spirit almost invariably we find action verbs employed: Jesus is *conceived* in the womb of Mary through the power of the Holy Spirit (Matt 1:18, 20); the Spirit *descends* on Jesus at his baptism in the Jordan (Luke 3:22); he is *led* into the desert for forty days by the Spirit and in the same power he returned to Galilee (Luke 4:1 and parallels); he *casts out* demons through the power of the Spirit (Matt 12:28); the Spirit will *sanctify* the disciples, and empower them to speak and witness to Christ. We should recall, however, that while being precedes action, action is what reveals being, and the fact that the Spirit is not always presented in

[2]For a good overall introduction to the Holy Spirit in Scripture and Tradition, see Alasdair I. C. Heron, *The Holy Spirit* (Philadelphia: Westminster, 1983).

[3]The Spirit is referred to in Mark 6 times, in Matthew 12, in Luke 17 (or possibly 18) in his Gospel, and some 57 times in his Acts, while in John we find 15 references.

personal terms does not negate the fact that the overall picture is one of personal presence. The Spirit, as it were, *personalizes* the divine power, the divine dynamism. Let us look more closely at some of the revealing actions of the Spirit in the life of Jesus.

In Matthew and, above all, in Luke, Jesus is *conceived* in the power of the Spirit, ". . . for the child conceived in her is from the Holy Spirit" (Matt 1:20b), thereby underlining his holiness right from the very first moment of conception. The Spirit is the womb in which the Son is born: "The Holy Spirit will come upon you and the power of the Most High will overshadow you; therefore the child to be born will be holy; he will be called Son of God" (Luke 1:35).

Mary and the Spirit have parallel roles, Mary fulfilling her role in a human way, the Holy Spirit in a divine way—and so Jesus is truly a human being, and truly the Son of God.[4] Indeed it is only when we take into account the dimension of the Spirit in Jesus Christ that we discover the vital dynamic relationship between the two natures of Jesus Christ, between his humanity and divinity. In the Lucan quotation above, notice the use of the word "therefore." It underlines the inseparable intimacy between the Spirit and the Son, as well as the dynamic nature of the Spirit. When we remember this, then we can understand why one of the special functions of the Spirit is to reveal Jesus precisely as the Son of God, and this is so because he is, as we have said, none other than the Spirit of the Son in his sonship. Again we are reminded that the Son and the Spirit are inseparable, and if we are to understand Jesus at the deepest level of his being, we can only do so in and through his Spirit.

In the mystery of the incarnation we have seen how the Father takes the initiative, but this initiative is taken *in* the Spirit, and Jesus is the Son of the Father, precisely because he has been generated by the Father in the Spirit. Because of this

---

[4]See F. X. Durrwell, "Pour une christologie selon l'Esprit Saint," *Nouvelle revue théologique* 114:5 (Oct. 1992) 653–77, especially 660.

Jesus is the one who incarnates in himself all the power and dynamism of the Spirit. All the Gospels describe his baptism at the hands of John and the descent of the Holy Spirit on him at that point:

> And when Jesus had been baptized, just as he came up from the water, suddenly the heavens were opened to him and he saw the Spirit of God descending like a dove and alighting on him (Matt 3:16; cf. Mark 1:10; Luke 3:2; John 1:33).

Notice here again the union of the ideas of the presence of the Spirit and the revelation of Jesus as the Son of God.

In Nazareth in what has been termed the inaugural address of his public life, Jesus proclaims: "The Spirit of the Lord is upon me . . . ." (Luke 4:18). Indeed, behind every activity of Jesus stands the Holy Spirit as the moving power. His life is Spirit-penetrated through and through. As James D. G. Dunn has written:

> Consciousness of a spiritual power so real, so effective, so new, so final, was the well-spring of both his proclamation of the divine "presentness" of the future kingdom and his authority in deed and word. This consciousness is summed up in the word "Spirit." His awareness of being uniquely possessed and used by the divine Spirit was the mainspring of his mission and the key to its effectiveness.[5]

It is impossible to understand the mystery of Jesus Christ apart from his relation to the Spirit. Separated from the Spirit Jesus could not be the Son of the Father, could not be God incarnate.

It is through the Holy Spirit that he works his miracles and casts out demons: "But if it is by the Spirit of God that I cast out demons, then the kingdom of God has come to you" (Matt 12:28). The Spirit is the dynamic power which causes the Kingdom of God to break through in this world. This

---

[5]James D. G. Dunn, *Jesus and the Spirit* (Philadelphia: Westminster, 1975) 54.

is an important point to remember for our own Christian mission in the world. (In the parallel passage in Luke, we find, somewhat surprisingly, given Luke's predilection for the Spirit, the phrase the "Finger of God" in place of "The Spirit of God." Perhaps Luke—or the original source—wished in this way to bring out the fact already referred to that the Spirit was conceived primarily as the medium of action of God, and from all accounts Jesus was very much aware that this power of God was active in his life.)

Another way in which Jesus shows the presence of the Spirit of God in him, and the fact that he is led in all things by the Spirit, is his freedom vis-a-vis the Law and the traditions of the ancestors. The Spirit of God is always a liberating Spirit; the spirits of the world, the spirit of the flesh are enslaving. Jesus preaches with power and authority—such that his listeners were continually amazed: "They were all amazed, and they kept on asking one another, 'What is this? A new teaching—with authority! He commands even the unclean spirits, and they obey him'" (Mark 1:27). In these ways the evangelists make clear to their readers that the coming of Jesus signifies the coming of the definitive salvation to humanity. He is the Anointed One, the Messiah, the one who bears the Spirit of God in his own being. And it is precisely because he is anointed with the Spirit that he is the Messiah: "God anointed Jesus of Nazareth with the Holy Spirit and with power" (Acts 10:38a).

However, it is in the resurrection that this presence of the Holy Spirit in Jesus is made fully manifest; it is here that his messiahship is revealed in all its perfection. Paul opens his powerful Letter to the Romans with the following words:

> Paul, a servant of Jesus Christ, called to be an apostle, set apart for the gospel of God, which he promised beforehand through his prophets in the holy scriptures, the gospel concerning his Son, who was descended from David according to the flesh and was declared to be Son of God with power according to the spirit of holiness by resurrection from the dead, Jesus Christ our Lord (vv. 1-4).

Since the Spirit, as the vital force within the divinity, is the Life-Giver (and it was precisely because the Spirit was perceived as a life giver that he was perceived as being fully divine), it is therefore proper to the Spirit to give life and that is why the event of the resurrection is appropriated to the Spirit in a special way. The resurrection shows that Jesus has now entered into a new form of existence, a new form of life—life in all its infinite perfection. The whole life of Jesus on earth was a gradual transformation into life in the Spirit, and this transformation is fully manifested in the resurrection. The humanity now totally transformed into the Spirit is capable of sharing the intimate life of God in all its fullness. Jesus in his dying and rising completes the final step in his journey from loving in a virtuous human way to loving in a way that is proper to the trinitarian divine life. And this transformation is effected from beginning to end *in the Spirit*. The heart of Jesus is now, as it were, totally transformed and submerged in the infinite love of the Father and the Son in the Spirit. The resurrection is the moment when the humanity of Christ is shown to have entered totally into the Spirit, into God, for, as the evangelist John reminds us, "God is Spirit" (4:24). The same evangelist on more than one occasion makes reference to this intimate connection between the resurrection and the Holy Spirit: "Now he said this about the Spirit, which believers in him were to receive; for as yet there was no Spirit,[6] because Jesus was not yet glorified" (7:39; cf. also, 20:21-22).

Consequently Jesus Christ has now left the sphere of death, the sphere of sin, and they have absolutely no power over him. By his death and resurrection Christ has broken the stranglehold of sin and death on humanity and taken humanity into the glorious freedom of the life of God. "He is risen" means that he is now in the sphere of this infinite, eternal, perfect Life, he is glorified, in "Glory." He is the "Lord of glory" (1 Cor 2:8) now reigning supreme. This is

---

[6]I.e., There was yet no outpouring of the Spirit among the Christian community.

the extraordinary marvel that is the paschal mystery, that in his death on the Cross and rising to new life in the Spirit, he has brought his humanity into the mystery of the life of the Trinity. That is why the resurrection is not just the recognition of the salvation gained by the Cross but is in itself its final stage. Jesus, our brother, like us in all things but sin, not only *won* salvation for us by his death and resurrection, but he *became* our salvation: "He [God the Father] is the source of your life in Christ Jesus, who became for us wisdom from God, and righteousness and sanctification and redemption" (1 Cor 1:30).

Just as the initiation of the saving process had its source in the Spirit, so likewise the concluding stage of that process has the very same source. Here we recall the image of Irenaeus of the Son and the Spirit as being the two hands of the Father[7]: the Father stretches out in love and life his two hands to all creation and in the plan of salvation, inviting all to enter into his life, share it and rejoice in it. The two hands, Son and Spirit, stretch out and gather us in. The two are present from all eternity with the Father, present in every aspect of creation, and present in every aspect of redemption. To speak anthropomorphically, the Father does nothing without his "hands!"

In the power of the Holy Spirit the mortal body of Jesus was transformed into a spiritual body in the paschal mystery, and according to God's plan of salvation this paschal experience of Jesus is to be communicated to all human beings:

> What is sown is perishable, what is raised is imperishable. It is sown in dishonor, it is raised in glory. It is sown in weakness, it is raised in power. It is sown a physical body, it is raised a spiritual body. If there is a physical body there is also a spiritual body (1 Cor 15:42-44).

This dying in the flesh to rise spirit is made possible by the Holy Spirit who wishes to communicate the same gift to anyone who is disposed to receive it. Pentecost is the culmination

---

[7] *Against Heresies,* Bk IV, pref 4; 20,1; Bk V, 1,3; 5,1; 6,1.

of the incarnation. Without Pentecost the plan of salvation would not be complete:

> When the work which the Father had given the Son to do on earth was accomplished, the Holy Spirit was sent on the day of Pentecost in order that he might forever sanctify the Church, and thus all believers would have access to the Father through Christ in the one Spirit. He is the Spirit of life, a fountain of water springing up to life eternal. Through him the Father gives life to men who are dead from sin, till at last He revives in Christ even their mortal bodies.[8]

For Christians this process of giving life begins with baptism and is effected gradually throughout one's whole existence here on earth through the sacraments of the Church:

> The Spirit dwells in the Church and in the hearts of the faithful as in a temple. In them he prays and bears witness to the fact that they are adopted sons. The Spirit guides the Church into the fullness of truth and gives her a unity of fellowship and service. He furnishes and directs her with various gifts, both hierarchical and charismatic, and adorns her with the fruits of His Grace. By the power of the gospel He makes the Church grow, perpetually renews her, and leads her to perfect union with her Spouse. The Spirit and the Bride both say to the Lord Jesus, "Come!" Thus the Church shines forth as "a people made one with the unity of the Father, the Son, and the Holy Spirit."[9]

But as Vatican II made clear, all peoples are called to share in it:

> Since Christ died for all men, and since the ultimate vocation of man is in fact one, and divine, we ought to believe that the Holy Spirit in a manner known only to God offers to every man the possibility of being associated with this paschal mystery.[10]

---

[8]*Lumen gentium* 4.
[9]Ibid.
[10]*Gaudium et spes* 22.

This reminds us of the words of Paul:

> Through him both of us have access in one Spirit to the Father
> (Eph 2:18).

The new life that we have received is at one and the same time truly *Christian* life—a sharing in Christ's life with the Father, and life that is *fruit of the Spirit:*

> The fruit of the Spirit is love, joy, peace, patience, kindness, generosity, faithfulness, gentleness, and self-control. And those who belong to Christ Jesus have crucified the flesh with its passions and desires. If we live by the Spirit, let us also be guided by the Spirit (Gal 5:22-25).

It is both life "in Christ" and "life in the Spirit." The overall picture of the Spirit that emerges from the pages of Scripture is that of an all-pervading presence, a presence that is found in the innermost heart of creation, in the deepest recesses of our being, sustaining all, giving life to all, loving all. This presence is revealed gradually down through the different stages of salvation history, and finds its fulfillment and most complete expression in Christ. The Spirit is none other than the "Spirit of your Father" (Matt 10:20) who at the same time is the "Spirit of Jesus" (Acts 16:17), or the "Spirit of Christ" (Rom 8:9).

This underlines the Trinitarian aspect of the whole plan of salvation as described in the New Testament. For the early Christians there was no such thing as a Christomonism, but rather a deep awareness that the one God, Father of all, revealed in Jesus Christ was totally involved in the work of our salvation. The whole plan could be viewed as the work of the Father, the work of the Son, and the work of the Holy Spirit. Very often we tend to look at the plan of salvation as developing along three stages: pre-Christ, Christ, post-Christ; there is a tendency to appropriate the first to the Father alone, the second to the Son alone, and the third to the Holy Spirit alone. But a careful reading of Scripture shows no such division. On the contrary, there we find that the three are intimately involved in each and every aspect of the history of salvation, from the first moment of creation to the parousia. In the plan each of the three Persons has their own characteristic role, without in any way breaking with the essential unity of their action. The Father begets the Son in the world and leads him into full filial relationship with him through the paschal mystery of death and resurrection. The Son in his human liberty submits himself in total and perfect obedience to the will of the Father in all things, and *thereby* reveals himself as begotten of the Father. The Spirit in the Father is the power of begetting, and in the Son is the power of being begotten. The Father is the origin and the terminus of the divine plan. Christ is the one Mediator in the descent of salvation from the Father to humanity, and in the ascent of humanity to the Father. The Holy Spirit is the ambient, the very "air" in which the whole plan from beginning to end is realized. The Spirit already at work in us here on earth gradually transforms us so that through Christ we can enter into the life of the Trinity.

The Trinitarian movement has its point of departure from the Father, through the Son but *in* the Spirit and in that same Spirit the movement is back to the Father through the Son. For that reason the Spirit is the bond between the Father and the Son, the personal reality in which the Father and the Son find themselves. And salvation is the insertion of humanity into this reality. When we keep this in mind we can better appreciate the dynamism of the plan in its entirety, better respond to the profound movement of love and communion which forms the very basis of the plan, and better appropriate the plan to our lives here below. When we forget the trinitarian nature of the plan of salvation, then we run the risk of misrepresenting the Christian faith regarding God and his dealings with humanity.

We too are begotten by the Triune God in the mystery of baptism, by means of which we are adopted by the Father as sons and daughters of God, incorporated into the reality of the Son, so that we form his Body, and regenerated in the Holy Spirit. And like Jesus we have to grow into the fullness of our belonging to God by allowing ourselves to grow in the life of

God in the Spirit, to let the Spirit bring us to the fullness of that life. Grace does not destroy our nature, but builds on it.

Jesus himself—especially as he is presented by John—is always deeply conscious of being in full communion with the Father in all aspects of the work of salvation. His food was "to do the will of the Father" and nothing else. Throughout his life on earth, as portrayed by the New Testament authors, Jesus is characterized by two aspects—one, that of being led by the Spirit in all things, and two, that of having a profound personal relationship with the Father, his "Abba." These two realities form the permanent threads out of which his life is woven, the threads that lead us back to his origin, and lead us forward to his glorification, the threads that help us to understand his life (and our lives as Christians) and his mission (and our mission as Christians).

We have seen that the immediate consequence of the resurrection was the complete and total anointing of the humanity of Jesus in the Spirit. Through his passover Jesus becomes definitively the Christ, *the anointed One,* anointed with the Spirit in an absolute, perfect, and definitive way, and as such he is now able to pour out his Spirit on all his brothers and sisters. Christ gives his followers his own Spirit. Now he not only becomes the supreme *revealer* of the Spirit, he also becomes the supreme *sender* of the Spirit. The pouring out of the Spirit on the Church is the "first fruits" of the harvest of salvation, the first fruits which are a token of what the whole harvest will be, and also the pledge and guarantee that it will take place:

> We know that the whole creation has been groaning in labor pains until now; and not only the creation, but we ourselves, who have the first fruits of the Spirit, groan inwardly while we wait for adoption, the redemption of our bodies (Rom 8:22-23).

The first action of the Lord portrayed by John as ascending into glory on Easter Sunday morning, and appearing to his disciples that evening, was to give them the Holy Spirit: "He breathed on them and said to them, 'Receive the Holy Spirit'" (John 20:22).

Christ himself had alerted his disciples that for their own good they must not become too attached to his earthly presence with them, but rather to his risen, glorified existence, made present to us through the Holy Spirit: "Nevertheless I tell you the truth: it is to your advantage that I go away, for if I do not go away, the Advocate will not come to you; but if I go, I will send him to you" (John 16:7).

The Spirit is the essential link between the glorified Christ in Heaven and his saving activity on earth. Without the Spirit the Church lacks the essential connection between humanity and the saving work of Christ. If the disciples would understand this, then they would rejoice for him that he goes: "You heard me say to you, 'I am going away, and I am coming to you.' If you loved me, you would rejoice that I am going to the Father" (John 14:28).

In Luke's Gospel, Jesus tells his disciples to wait for the Spirit in these words: "And see, I am sending upon you what my Father promised; so stay here in the city until you have been clothed with power from on high" (24:49).

And in his second volume he tells us that this has taken place: "Being therefore exalted at the right hand of God, and having received from the Father the promise of the Holy Spirit, he has poured out this that you both see and hear" (Acts 2:33).

Jesus Christ raised and exalted now possesses the Spirit in such a way that he can pour it out together with the Father on the community of his disciples, so that they too will now be "Spirit-bearers" just as he was while on earth; that they too will be guided in all things by the Spirit, just as he was; that they too will have this special relationship with the Father, "Abba," just as he did. Pentecost is the fulfillment of the Passover. With Pentecost the reign of God is fully inaugurated in the world. The promises made through the prophets are now fulfilled:

> For I will pour water on the thirsty land,
>   and streams on the dry ground;
> I will pour my spirit upon your descendants,
>   and my blessing on your offspring (Isa 44:3).

A new heart I will give you, and a new spirit I will put within you; and I will remove from your body the heart of stone and give you a heart of flesh. And I will put my spirit within you, and make you follow my statutes and be careful to observe my ordinances. Then you shall live in the land that I gave to your ancestors; and you shall be my people and I will be your God (Ezek 36:26-27).

In Pentecost the Spirit is revealed as God's eschatological gift to the world, a gift which made the Church to be the eschatological community. The Spirit is the soul of the Church animating her from within, making her one, holy, catholic, and apostolic,[11] empowering her to witness before the world of "the mighty works of God" (Acts 2:11), sending her forth to the world to proclaim the Good News. Through the gift of the Spirit at Pentecost the Church receives the same mission as Christ himself received, and through the power of the selfsame Spirit, is able to fulfill it. What the Spirit brings to the world is none other than the presence of our risen Lord and Savior. She communicates to us Christ's new, victorious, eternal life, his victory over sin and death, his sacrifice. That is why we are begotten as God's children through the power of the Spirit: "Very truly, I tell you, no one can enter the kingdom of God without being born of water and Spirit. What is born of the flesh is flesh, and what is born of the Spirit is spirit" (John 3:5-6).

This is the Baptism which Jesus gives: "I baptize you with water; but one who is more powerful than I is coming; I am not worthy to untie the thong of his sandals. He will baptize you with the Holy spirit and fire" (Luke 3:16).

The baptism of Jesus surpassed that of John as does the divine surpass the human. For Luke in particular, Christian baptism and the gift of the Holy Spirit were inseparable, and reception of the Holy Spirit was precisely the sign of full incorporation into the Body of Christ, into the Christian community

---

[11]See Yves Congar, *I Believe in the Holy Spirit,* II (New York: Seabury, 1983) 3–67.

(cf. Acts 2:11; 8:20; 11:17). But not only is the Spirit the source of our incorporation into Christ, the source of our adoption as members of God's family, but the Spirit is the one who enables us to understand and appreciate the mystery that overtakes us. The Spirit reveals to us the mind of Christ, helps us to enter into it, appreciate it, and savor it. It is the Spirit who leads us to the fullness of truth and the same Spirit who enables us to live within that fullness. The Christian life is consequently a *spiritual* life not just in a sense that distinguishes it from the physical life, or in the sense that we would refer to the life of piety of any religious person, alluding to, for example, the spiritual life of Moslems, or Hindus. For the Christian the spiritual life has a much deeper meaning in that we thereby allude to the fact that what constitutes its essence, its base, is none other than the Holy Spirit. The spiritual life of the Christian is, therefore, his or her whole life, in all its manifestations, moral, social, individual, economic, intellectual, physical, and material, all lived under the inspiration and guidance of the Holy Spirit. For that reason there can be no dichotomy for a Christian between the life outside of formal worship/prayer, and the life within it. The two are united, two manifestations of the one reality—the reality of the Spirit of God within the person.

The sacraments of initiation, especially baptism and confirmation, are the means by which we are incorporated into Christ and at the same time regenerated by the Spirit, and we thereby become Church. By baptism and confirmation we become God's adopted sons and daughters, commissioned to be his servants in the world and to the world. And what makes us to be his sons and daughters is precisely the gift of his Spirit:

> For all who are led by the Spirit of God are children of God. For you did not receive a spirit of slavery to fall back into fear, but you have received a spirit of adoption. When we cry, "Abba! Father!" it is that very Spirit bearing witness with our spirit that we are children of God (Rom 14:17).

Through baptism we are reborn in a very real sense, for we are given a new ontological being. Baptism signifies for us a new creation, and like Christ our birth is "not of blood, nor of the will of the flesh, nor of the will of man but of God" (John 1:13). Because of it each Christian can say in a very real sense, "It is no longer I who live, but Christ who lives in me" (Gal 2:20). What is mortal has been swallowed up by life (cf. 2 Cor 5:4).

Through baptism and confirmation in the Spirit the infinite gulf between the human and the divine has been bridged, and therefore there can be now real communion of life between the two. The immortal divine life can now flow into the veins of humanity and transform it, making it capable of entering into the very life of the Godself. Christ removed the barriers to the life of the Spirit in us, namely, our fallen nature, our sin and death. St. Nicholas Kavasilas, reflecting on this wrote:

> The Savior removed in succession the first by partaking of manhood, the second by being put to death on the cross, and the final barrier, the tyranny of death, he eliminated completely from our nature by rising again.[12]

Paul sums up the effect of Christ's life, death, and resurrection in the word "reconciliation":

> In Christ God was reconciling the world to himself, not counting their trespasses against them, and entrusting the message of reconciliation to us (2 Cor. 5:19).

> For if while we were enemies, we were reconciled to God through the death of his Son, much more surely, having been reconciled, will we be saved by his life. But more than that, we even boast in God through our Lord Jesus Christ, through whom we have now received reconciliation (Rom 5:10-11).

> For in him all the fullness of God was pleased to dwell, and through him God was pleased to reconcile to himself all

---

[12]St. Nicholas Kavasila (or Cabasilas—c. 1320–1391). This Byzantine mystic wrote an important work on the Christian spiritual life, entitled *The Life of Christ* (Migne, *PG* 150, 493–726). The quotation is found in, Panayiotis Nellas: *Deification in Christ* (Crestwood, N.Y.: St. Vladimir's Seminary Press, 1987) 111.

things, whether on earth or in heaven, by making peace through the blood of his cross (Col 1:19-20).

> For he is our peace; in his flesh he has made both groups into one and has broken down the dividing wall, that is, the hostility between us. He has abolished the law with its commandments and ordinances, that he might create in himself one new humanity in place of the two, thus making peace, and might reconcile both groups to God in one body through the cross, thus putting to death that hostility through it (Eph 2:14-16).

We associate the action of uniting, reconciling, with the Holy Spirit, for the Spirit is, so to speak, the bond of union between the Father and the Son. Thus it is proper to the Spirit to insert us into that union, thereby *sanctifying us,* and communicate to us the peace and reconciliation won for us by Christ on the cross. Through baptism the Spirit makes us sharers in the fruits of the perfect sacrifice of the Cross. So when Jesus speaks of giving us the Spirit, he speaks of communicating to us all that he has gained for us. Baptism sacramentalizes the gift of the Spirit as the one who regenerates us in the new life of the Risen Lord. Confirmation sacramentalizes the gift of the Spirit as the definitive, eschatological gift necessary for this final stage in God's plan of salvation.[13] In giving the Spirit he gives all, and that all is, in the final analysis, nothing less than participation in the divine life and that is salvation—to share in the glory of the Risen One. That is why salvation is much more entrance into something, rather than rescue from something. The Spirit is the Door through which we enter into the Way, the Truth, and the Life.

St. Paul sometimes refers to the effects of Christ's saving activity as justification. For example in his Letter to the Romans, he writes: "It will be reckoned to us who believe in him who raised Jesus our Lord from the dead, who was

---

[13]For a reflection on the relationship and distinction between the gift of the Spirit in baptism and in confirmation, see Liam G. Walsh, *The Sacraments of Initiation* (London: Chapman, 1988) 123–163.

handed over to death for our trespasses and was raised for our justification" (4:24-25).

Again we can see this very much in terms of the Spirit. Justification as Paul uses the word implies not just a mere legal fiction—God will look on us *as if* we are justified, but rather that Christians in and through baptism are really justified—we really are placed in a state of uprightness in the sight of God. God's Spirit transforms us radically, in the very roots of our being—and in this way he is indeed our "Paraclete," our "Helper" in a profound way. In this sense too the Holy Spirit is our Defender:

> When they bring you to trial and hand you over, do not worry beforehand what you are to say; but say whatever is given you at that time, for it is not you who speak but the Holy Spirit (Mark 13:11).

Calling the Spirit the "Advocate" underlines the Spirit's personal nature. The Spirit is not some unidentified, impersonal divine power or dynamism, but is the very bond of personal union within the Godself, a very powerful "power" indeed, the infinite power of the divinity, a power that is identical with love! When speaking about the Godself in its Trinitarian aspect, we are once more reminded that God surpasses all our categories in an infinite way. We are only trying to wrestle with truths for which there are no human cognitional models. The truths that we assert are rooted in the revelation of God, not in a merely human experience, and so we do not have control of the truths we handle—God has, and any insight we may gain into those truths is always a gift, a grace from him. We might too easily anthropomorphize our understanding of God if we only had revealed to us the Father and the Son, but the revelation of the Spirit, his presence among us, alerts us to the truth that God is infinitely more than we can ever express. In Jesus, we discover the God who reveals himself to us. In the Spirit we discover the God who is hidden.

CHAPTER 9

Christ, the Sender of the Church

In pouring out his Spirit on the first disciples Christ becomes in a special way the one who sends them out on their mission to the world. Without his Spirit it would be impossible for them to perform the mission, for it is none other than the continuation of his own mission: "As the Father sent me, so I send you." Vatican II in its Decree on the Missionary Nature of the Church *(Ad gentes)* brought out this point clearly:

> To accomplish this goal [the salvation of all], Christ sent the Holy Spirit from the Father. The Spirit was to carry out His saving work inwardly and to impel the Church toward her proper expansion. Doubtless, the Holy Spirit was already at work in the world before Christ was glorified. Yet on the day of Pentecost, He came down upon the disciples to remain with them forever. On that day the Church was publicly revealed to the multitude, the gospel began to spread among the nations by means of preaching, and finally there occurred a foreshadowing of that union of all peoples in a universal faith (no. 5).

Just as the birth of Christ at the incarnation was effected through the power of the Holy Spirit, so likewise the birth of the Church at Pentecost was effected through the power of the same Spirit. And just as the life of Christ and the mission of Christ were lived in the power of the Spirit, so likewise the life of the Church and the mission of the Church must be lived in the same Holy Spirit. We now, as the body of Christ, have been commissioned by Christ to continue here on earth his saving presence, his saving work. So once again we must return to the mission of Jesus in order to understand our own. Let us look at some of the characteristics of the mission of Jesus.

The mission of Jesus was universal.

At first sight this assertion may seem highly debatable. After all, his public mission as far as we know was directed exclusively to the Israelites and he himself said: "I was sent only to the lost sheep of the house of Israel" (Matt 15:24). However, it is important to remember that the context of this saying is none other than the encounter of Jesus with a non-Jew, the Canaanite woman, and the punchline of the story is the recognition and acceptance of faith by Jesus wherever it is found: "Woman, great is your faith! Be it done for you as you wish." And her daughter was healed instantly (v. 28).

Second, the whole approach of Jesus was indeed to the people of Israel, but that was the first movement; the second movement was to the rest of the world, either in and through the Jews if they accepted him, or without them if they rejected him, as indeed Israel as a nation did. It is difficult or perhaps even impossible to say what was the consciousness of Jesus in this matter. As a devout, believing Jew it would be most unusual for him to have an explicit consciousness of a direct mission to the Gentile world.[1]

However, the universal implication of Christ's mission lies not so much in his practice while on earth, but rather in the content of his message, in the *who* he was himself. The mission of Jesus was *to be* the perfect response of a human being to God the Father, and to reveal thereby God's relationship to his

---

[1]For a brief review of approaches to this question, see Donald Senior/Carroll Stuhlmueller, *The Biblical Foundations for Mission* (Maryknoll, N.Y.: Orbis, 1983) 141f.

creature and the creature's relationship to God. For that reason the universalism of the mission of Jesus springs from
within rather than without, from the core of the mission itself
rather than from any direct geographical injunction on the
part of the pre-paschal Jesus. One should not be surprised
therefore that it took the early Church some time to capture
the full force of the universal aspect of Christ's mission.

The writers of the New Testament had no doubt about the
universal significance of the Christ event—even though the
full realization of it was not achieved without tension and
difficulty[2]—and therefore of his mission, and they tried to
express it in various ways. For example, Mark opens his
Gospel with the words: "The beginning of the good news of
Jesus Christ, the Son of God." For him the Gospel was an
on-going process, a process inaugurated by Jesus Christ,
which continues in the Church and which will come to its
conclusion at the end of time. The Good News is something
that has as its core Jesus Christ, true son of man and true Son of
God, and this is vital for our understanding of the universality of
his mission.

Immediately after his baptism Jesus is once again proclaimed
Son of God: "You are my Son, the beloved; with you I am
well pleased" (Mark 1:11). Even the demons proclaim Him,
"the Holy One of God" (Mark 1:24). What is important is
that Mark presents Jesus in these universal terms, rather than
in terms that would tie him more directly to the specifically
Jewish context, such as Messiah, or Son of Man, or even the
Prophet of God.

In Mark Jesus is on a journey, on the way, a way that must
pass through Jerusalem and Calvary, and from there it will
extend to the whole world, and so as his Gospel story comes
to its conclusion, we have the words of the Risen Lord: "Go

[2]It is interesting to note that were it not for the determined leader-
ship of such people as Stephen and Paul, guided by the Holy Spirit, the
universality of the Good News of Jesus Christ might not have become
the reality of the apostolic Church as early as it did. Luke tells us that it
took a miraculous intervention to convince Peter of it! (Acts 10).

into all the world and proclaim the good news to the whole creation" (16:15). However, even before this there is a notable openness to the Gentile world, and there are many references to the universal missionary nature of the Christ event. For example there are two accounts of multiplication of bread (6:32-44 and 8:1-10). In the first, twelve baskets of left-overs are gathered (the number of the twelve tribes of Israel, the number of the apostles). In the second, seven baskets are gathered. Seven, like the first group of ministers chosen for the Hellenistic community, is sometimes interpreted as referring to the Gentile mission, seventy being regarded as the number of the Gentile nations (cf. Acts 6:1-7). And it is interesting that the bread which the Canaanite woman claimed for herself was the bread that was left over. Many of the crowd present, we are told, had "come a long way"—and many commentators see this as a direct reference to the non-Jewish world— and the disciples are instructed to share out the food among all. Everyone has the right to receive the bread of life.

Another very significant indicator of the universal reach of the Good News to be found in Mark's Gospel is the fact that it was the pagan centurion who recognized the true identity of Jesus at the foot of the cross (15:39): "Truly, this man was God's Son." For Mark, this is the goal of all Christian mission: to know and make known that Jesus of Nazareth is indeed the Son of God.

In Matthew's Gospel we also find this awareness of the universality within the mission of Jesus, and at the same time fidelity to the historical fact of the Jewish orientation of the actual ministry of Jesus. Matthew was obviously a great catechist, explaining his message with clarity and order. Matthew was probably a Christian Jew who had a thorough grounding in Greek and who probably lived in Syria. From Matthew we get a description of a true disciple of Jesus as one who identifies with him, imitates him. For that reason Christianity is more a style of life than a set of doctrines, and to be a disciple of Christ is to have listened to him and to have accepted his mission as one's own. For Matthew the Church, i.e., the community of those who believe in Jesus Christ, begins during the lifetime of Christ, with the call of the Twelve (10:1-9). For him, the Church is the continuation of the first group of disciples gathered around Christ, a community that lives in the presence of its Master and who carries on his mission:

> All authority in heaven and on earth has been given to me. Go therefore and make disciples of all nations, baptizing them in the name of the Father and of the Son and of the Holy Spirit, and teaching them to obey everything that I have commanded you. And remember, I am with you always, to the end of the age (28:18-20).

These final verses of Matthew's Gospel are the key to the understanding of the whole. The disciples have to do what Christ did, incorporate them into himself, thereby entering into the Kingdom and sharing in the promised salvation. A true disciple is a man or woman of faith, that is a person who lives out life in an attitude of confidence in Jesus and adhesion to his person, one who listens and constantly strives to understand the teaching of the Master and put it into practice. Baptism marks the beginning of this discipleship, and therefore the beginning of the mission of the Church, just as it marked the beginning of the mission of Jesus himself. Baptism is the moment of enlistment into the mission of Christ.

The two volumes of Luke—his Gospel and the Acts of the Apostles—have a profound intimacy with the mission of the Church. For Luke there is a movement out from Galilee, passing through Jerusalem, to the whole world. He traces the genealogy of Jesus right back past Abraham to Adam in order to underline his solidarity with the whole of our race. The mission to the Gentiles is described in the Book of Acts, but this is preceded in the Gospel by the sending out of the seventy,[3] and perhaps here again, as in Mark, it is not without significance that the number seventy was often in Judaism taken to be the number of the pagan nations.

---

[3]Some ancient mss. have "seventy-two." According to Genesis 10 seventy (seventy-two in the Septuagint) was the number of the nations of the earth.

Again in Luke 14:1-24 we have the theme of the banquet, which symbolizes participation in the Kingdom of God. Those who were invited did not accept the invitation and others are called to replace them. This is obviously a clear allusion to the refusal of the Jews and the mission to the Gentiles. This movement of presenting the Good News first to the Jews and then to the Gentiles is mirrored again in Acts. In the first twelve chapters we have the mission to the Jews, and the last twelve tell of the mission to the Gentiles. The intervening three chapters (13–15) form the bridge between them. The Book of Acts opens precisely with the Church waiting for the promise of the Risen Lord to send forth his Spirit so that his mission can be continued: "But you will receive power when the Holy Spirit has come upon you; and you will be my witnesses in Jerusalem, in all Judea and Samaria, and to the ends of the earth" (1:8).

From the beginning the Good News is announced to all, each in his or her own language (Acts 2:8-11), all are invited to conversion (Acts 2:39), and the salvation for which Christ was anointed (Luke 4:18) is offered to each and every one, especially the little ones, the weak, the sinners. Luke is very conscious that God has a preferential option for the poor.

Jesus continues his preaching ministry through the preaching ministry of the Church. To evangelize is constitutive of the apostolic Church, and as one writer puts it, "Any church that fails to reckon with this has missed a crucial component of apostolic Christianity, whatever else it may claim about its apostolic pedigree."[4] Luke was aware that the core of the preaching of Jesus was the Kingdom of God, and at the same time he was aware that the content of this phrase came to be manifest in the life, death and resurrection of Jesus. For that reason he sees the two as intimately united, and in closing his work on the mission of the Church with Paul in Rome—the center of the then known world—he chose these words:

---

[4]William J. Abraham, "A Theology of Evangelism," *Interpretation,* XLVIII 2 (April 1994) 117–30.

"He lived there two whole years at his own expense and welcomed all who came to him, proclaiming the kingdom of God and teaching about the Lord Jesus Christ with all boldness and without hindrance" (Acts 28:30).

The mission of Jesus is the revelation of the Father.

It is easy enough to understand what we mean when we say that Jesus is a true son of man, a fully human person with all that that implies. It is, however, not so easy to understand what we mean when we say that he is Son of God. God does not have a physical body, so God cannot have a son in the human sense of physical reproduction. Nobody understands the term in that sense. When we say "Son of God" we are using an analogy, a metaphor, derived from our normal human existence, to express what we see is the very special relationship between Jesus and God. For us the relationship between a human being and his or her father is an intimate, profound relationship. What we are trying to say when we call Jesus Son of God is that the human relationship points to it, is a metaphor for it, even though we believe that the relationship infinitely surpasses what we can conceive of or express in human terms. We must strive to keep in the back of our minds the analogical nature of our language when we talk about God.[5]

Jesus Christ is not just another great human figure with a message for humanity: Jesus is none other than God the Father with us, the eternal Father who has taken humanity to himself, so that in and through the humanity of Jesus Christ

[5]This is likewise of vital importance for a true understanding of inclusive language. Even though in practice it is difficult to implement inclusive language in our life and work, (especially in English), it is important for our understanding of God, and not merely out of sensitivity to modern sensibilities. To absolutize so-called masculine qualities, or refuse to acknowledge feminine characteristics, within the Godself is to impoverish one's understanding of God, and ultimately to have a false understanding of the divinity.

all humanity has access to the Father. We know that in every human being every other human being is in some way present—even modern science bears that out—but when that human being is also God incarnate then there is a whole different dimension. In the former dimension of our interrelatedness we keep on the horizontal orientation. When we enter into a relationship with Jesus we also enter into a profound relationship within the vertical orientation. It is our belief that only Christ in the communication of his Spirit can give us that profound vertical relationship with our heavenly Father and at the same time that profound horizontal relationship with all our brothers and sisters, and indeed, with all creation. And that is what the Church through the gift of the Spirit of Jesus is empowered to do. By her ministry of the word and sacraments she continues to reveal the Father's love and communicate the Father's life.

Jesus wished to continue his own mission through the Church.

We have already had occasion to refer to John's mission orientation when we spoke about his understanding of Jesus as the one sent by the Father, the supreme revealer of the Father to humanity. Jesus gathered to himself a group of followers, men and women who believed that he was indeed the one sent by the Father, the one who has "the words of eternal life . . . the Holy One of God" (John 6:68-69). This group of followers—the Church—is bound together precisely as a community of believers. Faith was the requirement for being a disciple: "Then Jesus said to the Jews who had believed in him, 'if you continue in my word, you are truly my disciples'" (John 8:31).

To believe in his word, continue in his word, was in effect to accept Jesus as the meaning of all life. This manifested itself in a life of love, and so faith and love are intimately connected: "By this everyone will know that you are my disciples, if you have love for one another" (13:35). In this way the disciples "abide in Jesus" and "my Father is glorified by this, that you bear much fruit, and become my disciples" (15:8). It is this "abiding in" Jesus that forms the basis for the identity in mission between Jesus and his disciples. It is for this reason that he is the sender of his disciples. We find this early on in John's Gospel. For example in 4:38 he presents himself as the sender: "I sent you to reap that for which you did not labor. Others have labored, and you have entered into their labor."

We find the same idea in 15:16: "You did not choose me, but I chose you. And I appointed you to go and bear fruit, fruit that will last, so that the Father will give you whatever you ask him in my name."

In these two passages Jesus appears as the absolute sender, without any reference to Father as we find in 17:18: "As thou have sent me into the world, so I have sent them into the world."

Also in 20:21: "Jesus said to them again, 'Peace be with you. As the Father has sent me, so I send you.'"

This underlines the parallel between his own sending by the Father and his sending of his disciples. The work of salvation is fully the work of the Father and fully the work of the Son. To separate the two in this is to be false to what has been revealed, it is to introduce a division where there is perfect unity.

And just as the sending of the Son by the Father is characterized by absolute trust and obedience to the will of the Father, so likewise the sending of the Church by the Son must be characterized by the same absolute trust and obedience. This is probably the reason why in John's Gospel there is in fact no sending forth of the disciples until after the resurrection. While he is on earth Jesus works alone with the Father (cf. 5:17, 19; 10:25, 32, 37), "the Father who dwells in me does his works" (14:10). Now with the Father in glory the work continues through the Church.

And not only must the mission be performed in an attitude of obedience and trust, it must also be exercised with deep humility. Jesus himself always manifested a deep sense of humility in the carrying out of his mission. We see this beautifully illustrated in his approach to the Samaritan woman before whom he presents himself as one needy and vulnerable.[6] He is the one who is "gentle and lowly of heart" (Matt 11:29), from whom we are to learn. Vatican II, in its decree *Ad gentes* expresses this point as follows:

> Since this mission continues and, in the course of history, unfolds the mission of Christ, who was sent to evangelize the poor, then the Church, urged on by the Spirit of Christ, must walk the road Christ himself walked, a way of poverty and obedience, of service and self-sacrifice even to death, a death from which he emerged victorious by his resurrection (no. 5b).

Paul, the missionary to the Gentiles, tells us in his First Letter to the Corinthians, that he went forth very conscious of his weakness, and "in fear and in much trembling" (cf. 2:1-5), and very much aware that "neither the one who plants nor the one who waters is anything, but only God who gives the growth" (3:7).

And if Jesus sends us forth to continue his mission of inaugurating the Kingdom of God here on earth, he also gives us the capacity to do so: "When he had said this, he breathed on them, and said to them, 'Receive the Holy Spirit. If you forgive the sins of any, they are forgiven them; if you retain the sins of any, they are retained'" (20:22-23).

The Spirit is the dynamic force enabling the Church to go forth and announce the Good News of salvation, witness to it with their whole lives, (Acts 1:8) so that the Father's design of saving all people in Christ may be fulfilled. It is the Spirit who develops and foments life in Christ, gradually bringing it to that point when "all of us come to the unity of the faith and of the knowledge of the Son of God, to maturity, to the measure of the full stature of Christ" (Eph 4:13). It is the Spirit who opens up the hearts of men and women so that they can accept Christ in the first place. Thus we have the

---

[6]On this episode see the beautiful and insightful commentary of Teresa Okure, *The Johannine Approach to Mission* (Tübingen, J.C.B. Mohr, 1988) especially 86–7.

fulfillment of the promise made during the Farewell discourse the evening before the crucifixion (cf. 14:16-17 and 16:6) is now fulfilled, and on the evening of the Resurrection the Holy Spirit is poured out upon the disciples by the Risen Lord. The fullness of this outpouring is manifested in the power to forgive sins.

Like Christ the Church must be guided by the Spirit and empowered by the Spirit in order to fulfill its mission of saving the world and glorifying the Father.[7] For John, the Spirit and the Church are intimately united, as are also the mission of the Church and the sending of the Spirit. They are but two aspects of the one reality. The coming of the Spirit on the disciples of Jesus Christ makes of them his Apostles. Without the Spirit the disciples were incapable of even initiating their apostolate, never mind carrying it through. We are reminded of this at the inauguration of Jesus' own apostolate on the shores of the River Jordan:

> And John testified, "I saw the Spirit descending from heaven like a dove, and it remained on him. I myself did not know him, but the one who sent me to baptize with water said to me, 'He on whom you see the Spirit descend and remain, this is he who baptizes with the Holy Spirit.' And I myself have seen and have testified that this is the Son of God" (John 1:32-34).

Everything that is given to Jesus for his mission is given to the Church for her mission:

> Now they know that everything that you have given me is from you; for the words that you gave to me I have given to them, and they have received them and know in truth that I came from you; and they have believed that you sent me (17:7-8).

---

[7]The Second Vatican Council affirmed on numerous occasions the centrality of the presence of the Spirit in the Church and in her mission. For example, *Lumen gentium*, 4, 12, 43, 45; *Dei Verbum* 5; *Gaudium et spes*, 1, 3, 11, 21, 23; *Presbyterorum ordinis* 12, 13, 17, 18.

The Church must seek only the fulfillment of the mission entrusted to her by Christ. All other motivations are foreign to her essential spirit:

> The Church is not motivated by an earthly ambition but is interested in one thing only—to carry on the work of Christ under the guidance of the Holy Spirit, for he came into the world to bear witness to the truth, to save and not to judge, to serve and not to be served (*Gaudium et spes,* no. 3).

In giving his Spirit Jesus gives everything. The Spirit is "the gift of God" (John 4:10) just as he himself is God's gift to humanity, the only gift capable of satiating our thirst for life, for truth in all its fullness. That is why Jesus told his disciples that the Spirit "will guide you into all truth" (John 16:12).

Throughout most of our Christian history Paul has been known as the Apostle to the Gentiles, and there is no doubt that if we are to understand Christ and his mission we have to go to Paul. Paul is the first writer chronologically in the New Testament corpus, and it would seem that his letters preceded the Gospels by some twenty or thirty years. In the light of this fact, it would perhaps have been more logical to examine his writings first. However, because Paul has relatively little to say about the life of the historical Jesus, it seemed best to leave him to last.

Paul's encounter with Christ and his response to him in a positive way are to be traced to his experience on the road to Damascus. This experience had four profoundly interconnected aspects:

1. Jesus is risen and lives now;
2. Jesus is the dynamic center of God's plan of salvation;
3. Jesus is present in all his brothers and sisters;
4. Jesus sends Paul to announce the good news to the Gentiles.

The last of these is a direct result of the other three. Because Jesus is risen a new and firm hope has dawned upon the world; because he is the center of God's plan of salvation then he has a universal significance. God's plan is one and Christ constitutes the center of that unity; without Christ there is no plan, and without him all the other aspects of the plan become ultimately unintelligible. Because he is risen, all who unite with him likewise share in his victory; because he lives now Jesus is profound good news for each and every human being and from that flows the obligation to go and proclaim that good news to a world desperately looking for meaning and hope and salvation. Paul had no doubt that Jesus Christ was for all:

> For I am not ashamed of the gospel: it is the power of God for salvation to everyone who has faith, to the Jew first and also to the Greek (Rom 1:16).

In the glorious chapter 8 of Romans, Paul proclaims the victory of Christ over the powers of evil, over sin and death, and this victory is achieved not just for himself, but for the whole world. "The law of the Spirit of life in Christ Jesus" is capable of setting us all free, "free from the law of sin and of death" (8:2). Paul's aim was to facilitate in so far as he could the action of the Spirit in all he met, a Spirit which enables each one to call out "Abba, Father!" (v. 15). He was deeply aware that

> the whole creation has been groaning in labor pains until now; and not only the creation, but we ourselves, who have the first fruits of the Spirit, groan inwardly while we wait for adoption, the redemption of our bodies. For in this hope we were saved. Now hope that is seen is not hope. For who hopes for what is seen? But if we hope for what we do not see, we wait for it with patience (8:22-25).

Love is the motive force behind this outreach—the love of God for us:

> Who shall separate us from the love of Christ? Will hardship, or distress, or persecution, or famine, or nakedness, or peril, or sword? As it is written, "For thy sake we are being killed all the day long; we are accounted as sheep to be slaughtered." No,

> in all these things we are more than conquerors through him
> who loved us. For I am sure that neither death, nor life, nor
> angels, nor rulers, nor things present, nor things to come, nor
> powers, nor height, nor depth, nor anything else in all creation,
> will be able to separate us from the love of God in Christ Jesus
> our Lord (8:35-39).

Paul's understanding of Christ and his understanding of mission are inseparable. If one really grasps the significance of Christ for oneself and for the whole world then the logical conclusion is to proclaim him to the world in some way or other, by the witness of one's life first of all, and secondly by the proclamation of Christ to the world where this is necessary. For God there is no distinction of persons, and all are called to the glory of belonging to God's intimate family.

> But now, apart from law, the righteousness of God has been
> disclosed, and is attested by the law and the prophets, the
> righteousness of God through faith in Jesus Christ for all who
> believe. For there is no distinction, since all have sinned and
> fall short of the glory of God; they are now justified by his
> grace as a gift, through the redemption that is in Christ Jesus
> (Rom 3:21-24).

For Paul what is essential is *faith*—faith that is the firm adhesion to the person of Jesus Christ, and that includes adhesion to his will: "For we hold that a man is justified by faith apart from works prescribed by the law. Or is God the God of Jews only? Is he not the God of Gentiles also? Yes, of Gentiles also, since God is one" (Rom 3:28-29).

Paul saw into the inner being of Jesus Christ and there discovered the fullness of the divinity and the fullness of humanity. From this awareness of who Jesus was everything else flows. For Paul what was vital was to know that Christ lived, died, and rose again. This does not mean that he was not interested in what Jesus taught, how he behaved towards others, what instructions he left with his disciples, what relationship he had with the God of Israel, with the law, etc.—all of these were important for Paul, but they had all achieved their highest expression in Christ's passion, death, and resurrection. We must not forget that in the Letters, we are not dealing with the actual missionary preaching of Paul but with his response to different pastoral problems that arose within Churches that had already received the preaching, either through himself or through other disciples (as in the case of his Letter to the Romans).

Paul never for a moment forgot that he was sent by the Lord Jesus, and over and over again he claimed full right to the title of "apostle" (cf. 1 Cor 9:1-2, 15:8-11). In the opening of almost all his great letters we find him identifying himself as an "apostle" (see Rom 1:1; 1 Cor 1:1; 2 Cor 1:1; Col 1:1; Gal 1:1). This obviously sprung from his Damascus experience. It was from Christ that he received the Gospel (Gal 1:12) and that revelation was made to him precisely that he "might preach him among the Gentiles" (Gal 1:16). For not only was he called to proclaim the Good News of Jesus Christ in a general way. He was also called to a specific way of performing that mission; he was to devote himself primarily to the non-Jews, the Gentiles.

Every Christian is called to continue the mission of Christ in his or her life. This is done by letting Christ live again through us—letting his thoughts be our thoughts, his way of relating to others be our way, his way of forgiving be our way—in a word, his way of loving be our way of loving. This is the fundamental and *sine qua non* of continuing the mission of Christ. However, there are times when the witness of life before others will need and require explanation—whether it be the witness of parents before their children, the witness of Christians before non-Christians, the witness of pastors before their flock, the witness of those specially called to preach the Good News to those who have not heard of it or have heard of it only very inadequately. Each of these are missionary situations in the true sense of the term, and it is only when this sense is fully assumed that the Church can truly grow and expand. This type of witness is necessary for her catholicity. Nothing or nobody must be excluded from her witness *a priori,* for the simple reason that the Church does not know where and how the Spirit is at work in each person, nation, or situation.

The Church is sent by Christ to continue his mission, and only when the Church—both local and universal—assumes that commission has she the right to call herself the Church of Christ. Paul reminded the Church in Corinth of her duty in these terms:

> All this is from God, who reconciled us to himself through Christ and has given us the ministry of reconciliation; that is, in Christ God was reconciling the world to himself, not counting their trespasses against them, and entrusting the message of reconciliation to us. So we are ambassadors for Christ, since God is making his appeal through us (2 Cor 5:18-20).

The more we discover Christ the more we discover what it means to be his followers, and just as in Christ his being and his mission are inseparable, so likewise with us: our being and our mission are inseparable. To be faithful to our baptismal being means being faithful to the mission we have received. In baptism we received the light of Christ—symbolized by the candle lit from the Paschal Candle, the Risen Lord—and that light is not only to show us our Christian way through this world and through the darkness of death, but also to enlighten the world. Jesus reminded his followers:

> You are the light of the world. A city built on a hill cannot be hid. No one after lighting a lamp puts it under the bushel basket, but on the lampstand, and it gives light to all in the house. In the same way, let your light shine before others, so that they may see your good works and give glory to your Father in heaven (Matt 5:14-16).

Jesus is the gift of God's life offered to each and every human being, and we are God's servants called to distribute that gift in the world. That gift coming from the Father is above all *life-giving* (is not the fundamental meaning of the word "father," life-giver?), and is life-giving for the whole world. For that reason Jesus is our certainty, the guarantee that what God wants, what God wills is that all have life, that all have salvation, that all find well-being and fullness. Jesus declares to us in what this well-being consists: participation in the very life of the Godself. But precisely because it is participation in *God's life*, we can never describe here below that life, and so "eye has not seen, nor ear heard, nor the heart of man conceived, what God has prepared for those who love him" (1 Cor 2:9). But we do know now that it is there, that it surpasses our wildest hopes, and that because of Jesus Christ it is present to and for us. That is the Good News we are sent to proclaim. This Good News is not the mere communication of knowledge but the establishment of a relationship with God and as such destined to perdure into eternity. Jesus is our definition of who God is, and of what God does for us. Our way to God is in and through him. Without Jesus there is no sure understanding of God, no understanding of salvation, no Good News. As Christians we have been commissioned to proclaim this to our brothers and sisters. That is in a special way the task, the challenge, the privilege, and the glory of the missionary.